ILLNESS, LONELINESS, and FRUSTRATION

ILLNESS, LONELINESS, and FRUSTRATION

EDWIN & LILLIAN HARVEY

HARVEY
Christian Publishers

UNITED STATES ADDRESS

Harvey Christian Publishers, Inc.
302 Jackson Street, Berea KY 40403
Tel./Fax (423) 768-2297
E-mail: harveycpbooks@gmail.com
http://www.harveycp.com

CALL BACK SERIES , VOLUME 1:
Illness, Loneliness, and Frustration

Cover & Content Design: John Shaffer

Printed by
Lightning Source
La Vergne, TN 37086

TABLE OF CONTENTS

CALL BACK SERIES, VOL.1

AUTHOR'S FOREWORD

SINCE BEGINNING this *Call Back series*, my beloved life-partner Edwin Forster Harvey and co-author of many of our books has been called to his heavenly Home. We had completed the first book in this series entitled *Illness* before his passing, and as I worked with Edwin on the subject of "loneliness," neither of us dreamed that bereavement would so soon separate the two of us who had prayed together, ministered together and written together as one for forty-five years.

With a heart torn by grief over my profound loss, I feel it to be God's will for me to prepare our unfinished manuscripts for the press. As I reread the jottings in Edwin's familiar handwriting, the tears are never far away. I am constantly reminded of the voice that is silenced here and the pen that can no longer challenge.

We begin this series with a "Call Back" from my husband, written shortly before his passing. May it and all the subsequent readings encourage, challenge and fortify every sincere soul that in their suffering, they may become, indeed, islanded in God.

I am also extremely grateful to Trudy Harvey Tait, Margaret Smith, Beulah Freeman and Edward Cook for their invaluable help in preparing these books for the press.

—Lillian G. Harvey, June, 1984

PUBLISHER'S FOREWORD

My HUSBAND and I are glad to present to our readers this compacted version of the first three books in the *Call Back Series*. My mother gave me full leeway to edit her writings after my father passed away which I have done only when absolutely necessary and for clarity's sake. To preserve space, we have omitted several readings from each book which did not deal directly with an individual's personal testimony. It is our desire that these writings will continue to bless many and be available to a larger audience through electronic versions. We hope to add two further volumes which will include the remaining books in this series. These volumes will also be available through print on demand with "Lightening Source."

Our prayer is that many struggling Christians will find strength and solace as they read of the struggles and victories of those who call back to us to follow in their path with joy, faith and perseverance.

—Trudy and Barry Tait, Oct. 2024

CALL BACK AND TELL ME!

Wherefore seeing we also are compassed about with so great a cloud of witnesses...let us run with patience the race that is set before us
HEBREWS. 12:1

Knowing that the same afflictions are accomplished in your brethren that are in the world
1 PETER 5:9

WHICH OF US struggling pilgrims has not, at some time or other, been perplexed, cast down or despairing until we have lifted some book and read the account of a saintly man or woman who bore suffering triumphantly? This has given us a renewed hope, a regenerated faith and a revived purpose because some Christian "called back" to us over the years, telling us that they too had endured illness, testing and opposition similar to what we ourselves were undergoing at the time.

Scriptural examples, of course, also produce mighty repercussions on us as we read them, but we are inclined to regard those divinely recorded sufferers as a special race of people. We forget that they all, like Elias, were people of like passions as ourselves. Biographies and testimonies of those not so far removed from us in time, however, produce limitless blessing. Our case does not seem unique; another trembling pilgrim has traveled this route! They have won through! They have learned the blessing of trial through their experience and call back to us, cheering us on in our similar pathway of trial.

The greatest inspiration of all, however, is the life of Christ, our Example. Alexander Maclaren speaking of Him says: "They tell us that in some trackless lands, when the friend passes through the pathless forests, he breaks a twig ever and anon, as he goes, that those who come after may see the traces of his having been there, and may know that they are not out of the road. And when we are journeying

9

through the murky night in the dark woods of affliction and sorrow, it is something to find here and there a spray broken or a leafy stem bent down with the tread of His foot and the brush of His hand as He passed, and to remember that the path He trod He has hallowed, and thus to find lingering fragrance and hidden strength in the remembrance of Him as 'in all points tempted like as we are,' bearing grief for us, bearing grief with us, bearing grief like us."

Call Back!

If you have gone a little way ahead of me, call back—
'Twill cheer my heart and help my feet along the stony track;
And if, perchance, Faith's light is dim, because the oil is low,
Your call will guide my lagging course as wearily I go.

Call back, and tell me that He went with you into the storm;
Call back, and say He kept you when the forest's roots were torn;
That when the heavens thundered and the earthquake shook the hill,
He bore you up and held you where the very air was still.

O friend, call back and tell me, for I cannot see your face;
They say it glows with triumph, and your feet bound in the race;
But there are mists between us, and my spirit eyes are dim,
And I cannot see the glory, though I long for word of Him.

But if you'll say He heard you when your prayer was but a cry,
And if you'll say He saw you through the night's sin-darkened sky—
If you have gone a little way ahead, O friend, call back—
'Twill cheer my heart and help my feet along the stony track.

—Unknown

EDWIN HARVEY
CALLS BACK

"By faith Moses,...refused to be called the son of Pharaoh's daughter; Choosing rather to suffer affliction...than to enjoy the pleasures of sin for a season; Esteeming the reproach of Christ greater riches than the treasures in Egypt."

HEBREWS 11:24-26

IT IS OFTEN ASKED: "How can a God of love often permit prolonged suffering to those who serve Him?" We reply that God Who allowed His beloved Son to pass through the most poignant suffering ever recorded, also permits His servants to endure because the blessed fruit of devoted suffering far outweighs the comparatively "light affliction, which is but for a moment." The blessings both to the sufferer and to others are very many. We would remind you of some of them.

First, Heaven-permitted suffering weans us from the entanglements of this vile world which are planned by the "god of this world" to result in our own eternal loss as well as that of others. By faith Moses chose rather to suffer affliction with the people of God than to enjoy the pleasures of sin for a season. So when we are struck with a severe blow that hurts to the inmost fiber of our being, let us "rejoice for great is our reward in heaven."

Then again, sorrow and affliction identify us with our Savior and draw us closer to Him. Indeed, they make us one with Him. We are now members of Christ "that is, of His body, the Church," and every blow struck against us is as if it were struck at Him.

> "Man may trouble and distress me;
> 'Twill but drive me to Thy breast.
> Life with trials hard will press me,
> Heaven will bring me sweeter rest."

It therefore follows that we, by suffering, are carrying on His divine purposes. "We fill up that which is behind of the sufferings of Christ." Of course, we cannot participate in the suffering that brought redemption. The spotless One alone carried that through to completion. But it is doubtless true that whether it be among the Hindus along the Ganges or in the slums of New York or London, it is the willing sufferer who manifests God's love and is thus enabled to lead sinners to his/her Master.

And let us remember that suffering is a refining process. "And he shall sit as a refiner and purifier of silver: and he shall purify the sons of Levi, and purge them as gold and silver." The dross of self-confidence, of lack of feeling for others, of shallow-mindedness, of blindness as to opportunity—all this and everything else that hinders the Christian from serving and being as his Master, is greatly altered by pain, sorrow or earthly disappointment.

"Happiness" is the grand object of natural man, but we here remind the reader that holiness is the goal God has for men. "He hath chosen us…before the foundation of the world, that we should be holy and without blame before him in love" (Eph. 1:4).

And so when Jesus died to justify us and reconcile us to an offended God, He also sanctified us by His suffering. "Wherefore Jesus also, that he might sanctify the people with his own blood, suffered without the gate. Let us go forth therefore unto him without the camp, bearing his reproach (Heb. 13:12-13).

"Have courage, soul of mine,
The path that you must keep
Is long and lone and steep;
But many thousand feet
Have passed this way before;
All through the vanished years
These stones were wet with tears;

If others knew this road
And bore their heavy load,
If others went this way,
You, too, can bear dark night
Until the morning light;
If others passed this way,
Have courage, soul of mine!"

—Mary E. Rock

BOOK 1

ILLNESS

THE MOTHER OF THE SALVATION ARMY CALLS BACK

Out of weakness were made strong, waxed valiant in fight.

HEBREWS 11:34

CATHERINE BOOTH'S LIFE story has often called back to us, personally, when we were sore distressed and the work we had undertaken seemed to be threatened by the powers of evil. Opening her biography was like a cooling compress upon a fevered brow as we read of the struggle she experienced in order to see men and women born again of the Spirit. Hers was not just a success story, but an honest confession of weakness in conflict.

Very few of Mrs. Booth's audience could possibly know that this dynamic speaker who seemed possessed with extraordinary energy, would often go home to lie down on a sofa in an agony of pain after undergoing the ordeal of public speaking. On the platform, she had stood with eyes flashing as she poured out her message. Reporters had sat spell-bound under her pounding logic and declared that she would have convinced the stoutest unbeliever. Her own daughter, listening to her mother's scathing denunciations of the sin of self-righteousness, marveled that any of the wealthy in her audience would return to listen to this truth-telling, compelling, Spirit-filled servant of God. But come they did, and many were brought to a convicting sense of need through her ministry.

Catherine Booth carried a frail and suffering body all through life. She had a weak spine, a heart complaint, overstrained nerves and, in her later years, cancer. Let us remember that she was also the mother of a large family and a major influence in the formation of the Salvation Army which endured world-wide ridicule and opposition from its outset. "I don't care about my body," she exclaimed during her last serious illness. "It has been a poor, troublesome affair. I shall be glad for it to be sealed up. Oh, I have dragged it wearily about."

In a letter to a friend, she further reveals her infirmity: "I know I ought not of all saints or sinners either, to be depressed. I know it dishonors my Lord, grieves His Spirit and injures me greatly, and I would fain hide from everybody to prevent their seeing it. But I cannot help it. I have struggled hard, more than anyone knows, for a long time against it. Sometimes I have literally held myself, head and heart and hands, and waited for the floods to pass over me. But now I appear to have lost the power of self-command to a great extent, and weep I must. The doctors say, 'Never mind. Regard it as one result of your affliction.' But this does not satisfy me. I know there is grace to overcome. And yet, there seems much in the Bible to meet such a state. Well, at present I am under, under, under; and for this very reason I shrink from coming to you or going anywhere else. I don't want to burden others.

"My dearest says, 'Never mind all these rubs and storms. Let us fight through all, in order to save the world.' To this I say 'Amen!' But one must have strength to fight. It is easier for some of us to fight than to lie wounded in the camp. I can neither fight nor run. I can only endure—oh, that I could always say, with patience!

"We are compassed with difficulties on every side. Still there is so much to praise God for, that I ought never to look at these troubles. Well, we shall pull through and get HOME! Then we will have a shout and a family gathering and no mistake!

"I feel about these troubles just as I do about my own health. When I pray about it, I am met with, 'Ye know not what ye ask.' I have such a sense of the wisdom and benevolence of God underlying every other feeling that I dare not go beyond, 'Nevertheless, not my will, but Thine be done.'"

How well Mrs. Booth had learned her lesson is shown in a letter written to advise and encourage another sufferer: "Try to rest in His will, dear friend, because there is nowhere else to rest. I am trying to do so. He knows why these wearisome months of suffering are appointed me, and amidst all my depression and sometimes distress, the devil shall not drive me from this one refuge—that He does it all in love. I know it, I believe it, and I pray that I may not frustrate His design."

"I return home" she writes after a visit to her doctor, "but little better in the main than when I came. So the time and expense seem to be thrown away, and I am useless still! The Lord reigns over death as well as life. The keys of death and hell are at His girdle.

"Try to get into that happy frame of mind to be satisfied if Christ be exalted, even if it be only by compelling you to lie at the foot of the Cross and look upon Him. If your happiness of soul comes to depend on the excitement of active service, what if God should lay His hand upon you and give you the cup of suffering instead of labor? Nothing but a heart in unison with Him and a will perfectly subdued, can give peace."

In his biography of his mother-in-law, Herbert Booth-Tucker gives us some personal insights into this amazing saint's endurance as she continued her ministry to others while suffering almost indescribable pain and discomfort:

"Scores of times she sallied from her sick-bed to face the eager, waiting crowds who hung upon her lips, and no sooner had she finished than she hurried back to it, utterly prostrated by the effort. Again and again she would be compelled, even while the meeting was in progress, to place the hymnbook in another's hands, rush into the vestry to relieve the nausea which even her iron will could not restrain, and then return to deal with penitents who little dreamed the anguish that her labors cost.

"It was a life-long martyrdom, none the less heroic because self-inflicted and avoidable. There was no need for an inquisitor to stand with rack and faggot in one hand, and recantation paper in the other.

Her weak body was its own inquisitor, but, overpowered, like her Master, with a sense of compassion for the shepherdless sheep, she would not surrender to its calls. Her indomitable determination carried her along. Like the British soldiers at Waterloo, she knew not when she was defeated; she fought when she should have rested, advanced when she should have retreated, lived when she should have died."

EDWARD PAYSON
CALLS BACK

Jesus said unto them…, can ye drink of the cup that I drink of?
and be baptized with the baptism that I am baptized with?

MARK 10:38

EDWARD PAYSON has been considered by his contemporaries comparable to William Bramwell in his effective prayer life, to John Fletcher in his holy living, and to Elijah Hedding in his triumphant death. Mr. Payson knew his Bible so well that it was said he could comment on every verse of Scripture. His intense ardor for souls was due to a baptism which he describes as follows: "God has pleased to fill me with Himself, so that I was burned up with most intense love and panting after holiness." His observance of long prayer sessions and fasting impaired his bodily strength so that he died comparatively young at forty-four years of age.

This saintly minister spent twenty years at a Congregational church in Portland, Maine. One would have thought he would have been one of God's favorites, exempted from suffering, but such was not the case as his own words reveal: "My flesh trembles and my blood almost runs cold when I look back on what I have suffered. A very large proportion of my path lies through the valley of the shadow of death."

On being asked, "Do you feel reconciled to this affliction?" he replied: "Oh, that is too cold; I rejoice; I triumph; and this happiness will endure as long as God Himself, for it consists in admiring and adoring Him. I can find no words to express my happiness. I seem to be swimming in a river of pleasure which is carrying me on to the great Fountain. It seems as if all the bottles of Heaven were opened, and all its fullness and happiness have come down into my heart. God

CALL BACK SERIES · VOLUME 1

has been depriving me of one blessing after another; but as every one was removed, He has come in and filled up its place; and now, when I am a cripple and not able to move, I am happier than ever I was in my life before, or ever expected to be. If I had believed this twenty years ago, I might have been spared much anxiety.

"If God had told me some time ago that He was about to make me as happy as I could be in this world, and then told me that He would begin by crippling me in all my limbs and removing me from all my usual sources of enjoyment, I should have thought it a very strange mode of accomplishing His purpose.

"And yet, how is His wisdom manifest even in this? For if you should see a man shut up in a closed room, idolizing a set of lamps and rejoicing in their light, and you wished to make him truly happy, you would begin by blowing out all his lamps and then throw open the shutters to let in the light of Heaven."

A friend once commented to him: "I presume it is no longer incredible to you that martyrs should rejoice and praise God in the flames and on the rack."

"No," said he; "I can easily believe it. I have suffered twenty times as much as I could in being burned at the stake, while my joy in God so abounded as to render my sufferings not only tolerable but welcome.

"God is literally now my all in all. While He is present with me, no event can in the least diminish my happiness; and were the whole world at my feet trying to minister to my comfort, they could not add one drop to my cup."

In a letter to a friend, this suffering Christian calls back, explaining why trials are necessary: "After all this, you will not wonder to hear that I am borne down with heavy burdens; pressed out of strength, above measure, so as, at times to despair even of life. All this is absolutely necessary and I desire to consider it as a mercy, but it is hard, very hard to bear. If anyone asks to be made a successful minister, he knows not what he asks. It becomes him to consider whether he can drink deeply of Christ's bitter cup, and be baptized with His baptism."

> Through much distress and pain,
>   Through many a conflict here,
> Through blood, ye must the entrance gain
>   Yet I disdain to fear.
> "Courage!" your Captain cries,
>   Who all your toil foreknew;
> "Toil ye shall have, yet all despise;
>   I have o'ercome for you."
>
> —Charles Wesley

CHARLES SIMEON
CALLS BACK

In that day shall the Lord of hosts be for...strength to them that turn the battle to the gate.

ISAIAH 28:5-6

VERY OFTEN in our lives, struggles and troubles do not come singly. Charles Simeon, an effective Cambridge teacher and preacher, experienced great inroads upon his health—no doubt a result of much opposition and hatred from both faculty and student body. There was indeed a long time during which his strength was so reduced that his public activity was curtailed, sometimes keeping him from Cambridge for many months at a time.

Early in 1807, after twenty-five years of intense ministry, he felt his health fail—in particular, his voice became weak so that he could preach only with difficulty and never more than once a day. After each sermon he found himself more like one dead than alive. Even conversation was often impossible, unless in a whisper. This condition lasted with variations for thirteen years, and then, at the age of sixty, it passed away quite suddenly and without any evident physical cause.

It is not surprising that this stricken servant of God would sometimes long for relief and in his mind had decided that at the age of sixty he would retire from his strenuous labors. This would be indeed a "Sabbath evening"—like entering a sea of calm during the evening years of his life! Now, suffering doubly from both outward opposition and inward weakness, it would seem that few of God's servants, humanly speaking, would have deserved this more. But God's ways are not our ways, and suddenly a truly miraculous event took place in his life which resulted in another thirteen years of most fruitful ministry.

He was on his last visit to Scotland in 1819, and just as he crossed the Border, he found himself, to his great surprise, "almost as perceptibly renewed in strength as the woman was after she had touched the hem of our Lord's garment." He saw in this revival of energy no miracle, in the common sense of the word, yet a distinct providence. It seemed as if his Master was saying: "I laid you aside, because you entertained with satisfaction the thought of resting from your labor—but now that you have arrived at the very period when you had promised yourself that satisfaction and have determined instead to spend your strength for Me to the latest hour of your life, I have doubled, trebled, quadrupled your strength, that you may execute your desire on a more extended plan."

"I do not approve," he says, as he looks back in 1820, "of fancying myself more an object of God's special care and favor than other people, and much less of recording any such conceit—but this particular interposition of the divine goodness I think I ought to see and acknowledge."

Through sunshine and rain, this rugged soldier of Christ's cross maintained a deep prayer life which was doubtless the secret of his triumph in the fiercest battles. He writes: "I find that an exceedingly close walk with God is necessary for the maintaining of fervor in intercession. Sometimes an extraordinary sense of want may beget fervor in our petitions, or a peculiar mercy enliven our grateful acknowledgments—but it is scarcely ever that we can intercede with fervor unless we enjoy our habitual nearness to God."

ROBERT MURRAY McCHEYNE AND JOHN HYDE CALL BACK

And they shall be mine, saith the Lord of hosts, in that day when I make up my jewels; and I will spare them, as a man spareth his own son that serveth him.

MALACHI 3:17

ROBERT MURRAY McCHEYNE, the Scottish David Brainerd, chafed under the command to rest: "Since Tuesday have been laid up with illness," he wrote in his diary. "Set by once more for a season to feel my unprofitableness and cure my pride. When shall this self-choosing temper be healed? 'Lord, I will preach, run, visit, wrestle,' said I. 'No, thou shalt lie in thy bed and suffer,' said the Lord."

Praying John Hyde, a missionary to India, misunderstood, at first, the frustrating illness which dogged him, compelling him to rest. He says, "I prayed, 'Enlarge my border,' with perhaps some temporal things much in mind and hope. The answer was an illness, straitening and limiting strength and efforts—taking me, keeping me from work for months, pressing home lessons of waiting, impressing the great lesson, 'Not my will but Thine be done.' But with the straitening came spiritual enlarging. How often God withholds the temporal, or delays it, that we may long for and seek the spiritual."

> "Just set aside," I hear Thy sweet voice whisper,
> "Just set aside, that you may come to know
> That fuller, deeper, still and sweet communion
> So often missed while hurrying to and fro."
>
> Just set aside! It seems a strange procedure,
> Just set aside when life is at its best;
> There is no choice, though service would be sweeter,
> Just gently, firmly, set aside to rest.

Just set aside! Dear God, I tried to serve Thee,
    And though I played a small, important part,
And, eager still…but what have I to give Thee?
    Just set aside, I lean against Thy heart.

"Just set aside" I hear Thy sweet voice whisper,
    "Just set aside, that you may come to know
That fuller, deeper, still and sweet communion
    So often missed while hurrying to and fro."

Just set aside! No longer now impatient,
    I drink with joy the rivers of Thy grace;
Surrounded by Thy love I am contented,
    For I have glimpsed anew Thy precious Face.

Just set aside in holy, sweet communion,
    Just trusting when I do not understand;
Just set aside…perhaps to serve Thee better,
    Just waiting in the hollow of Thy Hand.

—Alice Hansche Mortenson
USED BY PERMISSION

FRANCES RIDLEY HAVERGAL CALLS BACK

No chastening for the present seemeth to be joyous, but grievous:
nevertheless afterward it yieldeth the peaceable fruit of righteousness
unto them which are exercised thereby.

HEBREWS 12:11

"WHAT THOUSANDS have blessed Him for the pain that came like a rough hand catching them as they fell over a precipice, hurting and pinching their very flesh but saving their lives! In how many ways a skillful doctor gives pain that he may prevent much greater and worse suffering! At the same time, I am quite sure that with very rare exceptions, bodily pain, though far more trying to witness, is not anything to compare with mental pain, and it leaves no sting or scar as almost every other form of every real trial must do."

These words were spoken by the author and poet, Frances Ridley Havergal. They sprang from the abundance of her own experience, for her doctors had declared that she was far more sensitive to physical pain than the average person. Though greatly used of God both through public speaking and writing, she was set aside for long periods because of illness and nervous exhaustion and she shares with all sufferers the lessons she learned from these experiences:

"Pain, as to God's own children, is, truly and really, only blessing in disguise. It is but His chiseling, one of His graving tools, producing the likeness to Jesus for which we long. I never yet came across a suffering (real) Christian who could not thank God for pain! Is not this a strong and comforting fact? I do not say that they always do so during the very moments of keenest pain, though much more often than not, I think they are able to do this; but, certainly, they do deliberately praise Him for it afterwards.

"I think one must pass through it for one's self before one can fully realize the actual blessedness of suffering. Meanwhile, you may well take the testimony of those who have. Its conscious effects are to give one deeper feeling of one's entire weakness and helplessness (a lesson which we are all slow to learn in health), and of the real nothingness of earthly aims and comforts and the fleetingness and "unsatisfactoriness" of everything except God. Then, it drives one to Him each moment; one cannot bear it even one moment alone; one must lean and cling.

"Then one has opportunities which one could not otherwise have of learning trust, and patience, and meekness; it is a time of growing up into Him in these things. Then, one realizes more what it must have been to Jesus to endure real, actual, bodily pain for us. I never saw such tremendous force in 1 Peter 2:24, 'in his own body' as when suffering great pain myself. It seemed a new page of His love unfolded to me.

"So far, the whole question of pain is rather one of sight than of faith to me now. It has become so clear to me, as a part of God's great plan which could not be done without. But I find yet scope for faith beyond. I believe there is a mysterious connection between suffering here and actual capabilities of enjoyment hereafter and that service above, to which I delight to look forward.

> "I take this pain, Lord Jesus,
>   From Thine own hand,
> The strength to bear it bravely
>   Thou wilt command.
> I am too weak for effort
>   So let me rest,
> In hush of sweet submission,
>   On Thine own breast.

"I take this pain, Lord Jesus,
      As proof indeed
That Thou art watching closely
      My truest need:
That Thou, my Good Physician,
      Art watching still;
That all Thine own good pleasure
      Thou wilt fulfill.

"'Tis Thy dear hand, O Savior
      That presseth sore,
The hand that bears the nail-prints
      Forevermore.
And now beneath its shadow,
      Hidden by Thee,
The pressure only tells me
      Thou lovest me."

—Frances Ridley Havergal

Summing up God's purpose in suffering, Frances Havergal calls back to us today: "I look at trial and training of every kind in this light, not its effect upon oneself for oneself, but in its gradual fitting of me to do the Master's work. So, in very painful spiritual darkness or conflict, it has already comforted me to think that God might be leading me through strange dark ways, so that I might afterward be His messenger to some of His children in similar distress. My ill health this summer has been very trying to me. I am held back from much I wanted to do in every way, and have had to lay poetizing aside. And yet such open doors seemed set before me. Perhaps this check is sent that I may consecrate what I do more entirely. I have a curious vivid sense, not merely of my verse faculty in general being given me, but also of every separate poem or hymn, nay every line, as a direct gift, not a matter of effort, but purely involuntarily ....

"I suppose that God's crosses are often made of most unexpected and strange material. Perhaps trial must be felt keenly, or it would not be powerful enough as a medicine in the hands of our beloved Healer; and I think it has been a medicine to me latterly."

The Lord will strengthen him upon the bed of languishing: thou wilt make all his bed in his sickness (Psa. 41:3).

EVA VON WINKLER
CALLS BACK

They...were forbidden of the Holy Ghost to preach the word in Asia,
After they were come to Mysia, they assayed to go into Bithynia: but
the Spirit suffered them not.

ACTS 16:6-7

THE CALL TO ENDURE tribulation for Christ in order to work with the sick and destitute came to Eva von Winkler when she was only seventeen. Her home was a beautiful old castle in Upper Silesia where culture, refinement and wealth had surrounded the young heiress from birth. Eva's father, rather disturbed with his young daughter's break with tradition and conventionalities, worried that she might be acting upon an impulse rather than upon deep personal convictions. He therefore withheld his permission for such a venture for several years which, understandably, was a trial to the young enthusiast for Christ. Eventually, however, Eva's father erected a small building in which she could house a few of the most needy.

The way ahead now stretched out before her with no apparent obstructions or detours. Other young women, attracted by Eva's devotion, joined her in her venture and she was all set to expand their accommodations. It seemed as if providence had turned all lights to green along the road on which this dedicated young pilgrim was to travel.

Then suddenly, Eva was called to a halt before one of God's unexpected red lights. Someone has said that "the stops of a good man were ordered of the Lord, as well as the steps." Exhaustion from overwrought nerves and affected lungs demanded imperative action. Her pastor who had been her old friend and advisor warned: "You may only have five years more to live if you continue without a break."

So she submitted to being carried off to his large institution for the sick at Bielefeld where she had formerly trained. The elderly pastor appreciated Eva's great gift for leadership and wished that she would join his institution permanently in that capacity, but the work was far too heavy for her frail shoulders. A more complete breakdown necessitated her removal to a more secluded spot.

Fred Brooks aptly describes these "detours" from what we consider our path of service:

> Side-tracked, my Lord, amid some pain and loss,
>   Unfit to strive amid the lab'ring throng,
> Weakened and spent—yet whatso'er the cross,
>   Resting in Thee, Who art forever strong.

This detour lasted for seven long years, but when Eva eventually rejoined her faithful helpers at Friedenshort, she recognized the purpose and plan of God in all of this. She saw the danger of "sinking into a rut of duties in a so-called Christian work, and missing the highest." "These years of learning," she remarked, "were necessary to prepare me for His service. In eternity we will praise Him for all the way He had led us and most of all for that which seemed hardest."

So again, the light was green for the long stretch of road ahead. Revival had come to this little group of "Sisters of the Poor" as they came to be called and had brought enlargement and development. Buildings were erected and the sisterhood increased by twenty and then by fifty a year. A deaconess order came into being and a committee was formed. But a new difficulty arose. Their source of income had been the interest on an inheritance from Eva's mother which was now exhausted, and the Sisterhood was faced with stepping out on faith alone. As funds diminished and expenses exceeded their income, the Committee opposed taking the next step by faith alone, and so it was disbanded and a new one formed which sympathized with its founder.

Another detour loomed ahead, however, this time of eighteen months' duration. Affected lungs with accompanying exhaustion once more laid Sister Eva aside and she had to learn that God did not so much desire her work as her loving attention—sitting at His feet, learning the secrets which would enable her work to be truly Bible-based. On this detour, Sister Eva met with Mrs. Baxter whose life of restfulness, trust and victory appealed to the over-tired worker who discovered that her output had exceeded her intake spiritually. Holiness of heart now became her quest and she hungered for the best.

Later in life, Sister Eva was again laid aside for eight months when she was called to hush her over-busy spirit into listening for the Master and building everything according to the pattern on the Mount.

We quote further from Fred Brook's poem:

> Side-tracked means this—a quiet time with God,
> Where no rebuffs nor "fearings" can alarm:
> A sweet content He breathes and lifts my load
> And shelters from the dangers that would harm.
>
> If once again, amid life's throng I move,
> With strength renewed and armed for the fray;
> I'll witness to the faithfulness I prove,
> And at His feet Love's greatest homage lay.

DAVID BRAINERD
CALLS BACK

That no man should be moved by these afflictions: for yourselves know that we are appointed thereunto. For verily, when we were with you, we told you before that we should suffer tribulation

1 THESSALONIANS. 3:3-4

FEW VOICES call back more clearly across the miles and over the years than does that of the slowly dying, pain-racked David Brainerd, fearless missionary to the North American Indians! During his lifetime, his voice reached the shores of England and arrested the attention of John Wesley, born the same year as himself but destined to live eighty-eight years as contrasted with Brainerd's brief life-span for he died before he was thirty. As he perused Brainerd's diary, John became deeply affected by the writer's prayer life—the lonely watches, the panting after holiness, the days of exhausting travel in spite of constant weakness, the pain-filled nights—and consequently, he urged his preachers not only to study it too, but to follow the example of this intrepid, pioneer missionary.

The young missionary's Spirit-amplified voice also echoed through the corridors of Cambridge University and was heard by a Senior Wrangler, Henry Martyn. This "voice" eventually took Martyn to India and later to Persia and encouraged him in his life of prayer and endurance in suffering. Martyn died young, and in both life and death, his voice, like Brainerd's, continues to echo down through the centuries, encouraging us to a life of devotion and service

Brainerd's "call back" was also heard in a shoe-shop in the English Midlands and helped to inspire William Carey to surmount all kinds of difficulty in order to go to India. Carey, in turn, calls back to us from the shores of that land.

If it had not been for a disappointment in the life of David Brainerd, we might never have heard of him. During a time of revival at Yale University, he was conversing with other students and was overheard deploring the spiritual condition of a member of the faculty. This seemed reason enough for the faculty to expel him, although he had been an excellent student. He was, however, duly ordained a minister and answered a definite call to preach to the Indians.

Brainerd confided to his journal a description of his field of labor: "The presence of God is what I want. I live in the most lonely, melancholy desert about eighteen miles from Albany. I board with a poor Scotchman; his wife can talk scarce any English. My diet consists mostly of hasty pudding, boiled corn and bread baked in the ashes and sometimes a little meat and butter. My lodging is a little heap of straw laid upon some boards a little way from the ground for it is a log room without any floor that I lodge in. My work is exceedingly hard and difficult; I travel on foot a mile and a half, the worst of ways, almost daily and back again for I live so far from my Indians. I have not seen an English person in this month. These, and many other circumstances, equally uncomfortable, attend me. The Lord grant that I may learn to 'endure hardness, as a good soldier of Jesus Christ!'

"My circumstances are such that I have no comfort of any kind but what I have in God. I have no fellow-Christian to whom I may unbosom myself, or lay open my spiritual sorrows; with whom I may take sweet counsel in conversation about heavenly things and join in social prayer."

Jonathan Edwards, Brainerd's friend and contemporary, tells us: "Brainerd's life shows the right way to success in the work of the ministry. He sought it as a resolute soldier seeks victory in a siege or battle, or as a man that runs a race for a great prize. Animated with love to Christ and souls, how did he labor always fervently, not only in word and doctrine, in public and private, but in prayers day and night!"

His doctor's verdict, "six months to live," must have been very disturbing to one so young. Instead of saving his life, however, Brainerd turned his face back toward the lonely wilderness and to the Indians until, at last, forced to retire, he found a refuge in the Edwards' home where he spent his last days. A few entries from his diary acquaint us with his labors during those last months:

"Sept. 28. Rode to my people, and though under much weakness, attempted to preach. Discoursed about half-an-hour at which season divine power seemed to attend the Word; but, being extremely weak, I was obliged to desist. After a turn of faintness, with much difficulty I rode to my lodgings, where betaking myself to my bed, I lay in a burning fever and almost delirious for several hours, till towards morning, my fever went off with a violent sweat. I have been feverish and unable to rest quietly after preaching; but this was the most severe, distressing turn that ever preaching brought upon me.

"Oct. 19. Was scarcely able to do anything at all in the week past, except that on Thursday I rode out about four miles; at which time I took cold. And I was able to do little or nothing so that I enjoyed not much spirituality or lively spiritual affection. Was composed and comfortable, willing either to die or live; but found it hard to be reconciled to the thoughts of living useless. Oh that I might never live to be a burden to God's creation, but that I might be allowed to repair home when my sojourning work is done!"

MARTHA SNELL NICHOLSON CALLS BACK

Out of much affliction and anguish of heart
I wrote unto you with many tears.

2 CORINTHIANS 2:4

"Looking back over nearly a lifetime of illness, I am thanking God for these pain-filled years," said Martha Snell Nicholson, best known for her inspiring poetry. So taxing and severe had her affliction been that her body had shrunk from five-feet-six to four-feet-eight and she weighed less than eighty pounds. Her spine had become so completely ankylosed (abnormally stiffened) that it was encased in a heavy steel brace. Her own words will best describe the secret of her serenity of spirit and cheerfulness that overflowed into song:

"When I stood at the beginning and strained my eyes to see down the dim path ahead, I was sure it would be strewed with roses. When pain and sorrow came, I could not understand, but now as I look back the long road which lies so clearly behind me, I see that His hand was upon me all the way.

"Never strong as a child, I broke down very early in young womanhood. I spent the ensuing seven years in bed, most of the time with TB, then up off and on, one sick spell after another, seven operations besides fifteen minor "carvings." It seems that almost every disease has had a try at me. For the last twenty years I have been on the shelf, able to attend church only once during that period.

"They have brought me gifts—those weary years. I do not enjoy sickness or suffering, or the nervous agony and exhaustion that are harder to bear than physical pain. And an invalid must bury so many dear dreams which have death struggles and refuse to die decently and quietly. But God has a way of taking away our toys, and after we have cried for a while like disappointed children, He fills our hands with jewels, which 'cannot be valued with the gold of Ophir, with the precious onyx, or the sapphire.'

"I recall that after I had been sick for several years, I thought, in my foolishness, that I had learned the lessons which God wanted to teach me, and that He would let me go out into the world and work for Him. As though one could ever learn all that God has to teach! No, I am still sick. I do not understand why I must still be an invalid. I no longer expect to understand. If I did, there would be no need for faith. Enough that He knows why, and some day He will tell me about it— why it was best for me and best for His cause.

"Then came the hardest blow of all. Nearly nine years ago, He called my beloved husband and left me here alone, crippled with arthritis, facing cancer, and with dimming eyesight and other illness into which I need not go. Then indeed I learned about God and that His strength is made perfect in weakness and that He can supply all my needs 'according to His riches in glory by Christ Jesus.' It is one thing to think so—it is another thing to have found out by actual experience that it is so, to know beyond a shadow of a doubt that when you go down into the valley, you can clasp His hand—that you never need to be alone or afraid for He will go with you on all your paths—and that His arm is strong enough to carry you. It is blessed beyond words to know these things."

Before she was called Home, Martha Snell Nicholson experienced an even more crippling form of illness—Parkinson's disease. Out of her suffering was born her poem entitled, "Tranquility."

> "The Hand which flung the stars through space
> Holds fast my hand.
> My life is molded by the One
> Who shaped the land.

The Mind which planned the march of suns
Can understand
The petty trials of my day;
Who hollowed out the cup that holds
The mighty sea,
And keeps the waves in check, can give
Tranquility
In my small storms. Shall not the One
Who holds in place
The Milky Way, keep me each day
And by His grace
Present me perfect, faultless there
Before His face?"

Martha Nicholson calls back to other sufferers and reveals what gave her courage to face the future:

"But the best part of all is the blessed hope of His soon coming. How I ever lived before I grasped that wonderful truth, I do not know.... Each morning I think with a leap of the heart, 'He may come today!' and each evening, 'When I awake, I may be in glory.' Each day must be lived as though it were to be my last, and there is so much to be done, to purify myself, and to set my house in order. I am on tiptoe with expectancy. There are no more gray days for they are all touched with color; no more dark days for the radiance of His coming is on the horizon; no more dull days with glory just around the corner—and no more lonely days, with His footsteps ever coming nearer, and the thought that soon, soon, I shall see His blessed face and be forever through with pain and tears!"

—*Wesleyan Advocate*
USED BY PERMISSION

RICHARD BAXTER
CALLS BACK

When Rehoboam had established the kingdom, and had strengthened himself, he forsook the law of the Lord, and all Israel with him.

2 CHRONICLES 12:1

He was marvelously helped, till he was strong. But when he was strong, his heart was lifted up to his destruction.

2 CHRONICLES 26:15-16

RICHARD BAXTER, the godly Puritan minister, suffered pain as a result of a kidney complaint which caused him to live every day as if it were his last. "O God," he prayed, "I thank Thee for a bodily discipline of eight-and-fifty years." In fact, he attributed his success in the ministry to the fact that he daily preached as a dying man to dying men.

Of one illness he commented: "Oh, healthful sickness! Oh, comfortable sorrow! Oh, gainful loss! Oh, enriching poverty! Oh, blessed day that I was afflicted! While I was in health, I had not the least thought of writing books, or of serving God in any more public way than preaching. But when I was weakened with great bleeding, and left solitary in my chamber at Sir John Cook's in Derbyshire, without any but my servant about me, and was sentenced to death by the physician, I began to contemplate more seriously on the everlasting rest which I apprehended myself to be just on the borders of. That my thoughts might not too much scatter in my meditation, I began to write something on that subject, intending but the quantity of a sermon or two. But being continued long in weakness, where I had no books and no better employment, I followed it on till it was enlarged to the bulk in which it is published."

It seemed strange that when true preachers of the Gospel were so much needed that this godly minister should be laid aside, but his biographer remarked: "If he had never written another book, it alone (*Saint's Everlasting Rest*) would have endeared his memory forever to all who cherish the sublime hopes of the Gospel." Thus his thoughts were preserved for us in print whereas his many sermons are forgotten.

"Weakness and pain," he remarked, "helped me to study how to die; that set me to studying how to live; and that on studying the doctrine from which I must fetch my motives and comforts. Beginning with necessities, I proceeded by degrees, and now I am going to see that for which I have lived and studied."

"Prosperity hath its peculiar temptations," he wrote on another occasion, "by which it hath foiled many that stood unshaken in the storms of adversity. The tempter who hath had you on the waves, will now assault you in the calm; he hath his last game to play upon the mountain, till nature cause you to descend. Stand this charge, and you win the day."

> Thank God for pain!
> No tear hath ever yet been shed in vain,
> And in the end each sorrowing heart shall find
> No curse, but blessings in the hand of pain;
> Even when He smiteth, then is God most kind.
> Thank God for pain!
>
> —Anon.

FRANCIS ASBURY
CALLS BACK

*For we which live are alway delivered unto death for Jesus' sake,
that the life also of Jesus might be made manifest in our mortal flesh.*

2 COR. 4:11

*In weariness and painfulness, in watchings often, in hunger and
thirst, in fastings often, in cold and nakedness.
Beside...the care of all the churches*

2 COR. 11:27-28

THE HIGH COST of spreading the good news of the Gospel in America
by early Methodist itinerants was appalling. If the cause had not been
so great, the seeming waste of manpower would have been a tragedy,
for the average lifespan of the pioneer ministers was only thirty-five
years. Beside some swollen stream, clothes soaked and body chilled
in death, the form of a preacher might be found. Oft times word would
leak through that the Indians had come upon some lone itinerant and
found him easy prey.

Bishop Francis Asbury was a courageous man who led the way
and never asked of his men that which he did not exact from himself.
This Englishman spent his early years not far from the bustling city of
Birmingham in the Midlands of England. Then the Lord wrought upon
his heart, calling him to toil on other shores. He has been called "The
Prophet of the Long Road," for he had no home in that vast wilderness
of colonized America. His incessant travels took him down lonely trails,
across chasms deep, over mountains and across swollen rivers where
no bridges had as yet been erected. His biographer, acquainted with
Asbury's journal, can best describe the inconveniences he suffered:

"He (Francis Asbury), journeyed when he 'had a kind of chill and headache'; he 'went' more than six hundred miles 'with an inflammatory fever and fixed pain in his breast'; and he traveled for a period of four months during which he was continuously ill and covered 'not less than three thousand miles.' He 'went' when he had a boil on his face and another on his eye; when his leg was inflamed; when his 'breast was inflamed'; when he had influenza; when he had 'a putrid sore throat'; when he was so ill he had no appetite'; when he had a toothache; when he had a high fever; when he was so weak that he was ready to faint; when he was in pain from head to foot; when he had a running blister on his side; when he was so ill that, to him, death would have been welcome; when he had only strength enough to write in his Journal 'Pain, Pain, Pain'; through rain and snow, through drought and dust, without food, without drink, over mountains, through deep rivers and muddy creeks, on, on, on, day after day, month after month, year after year, one decade, two, three, four decades, until he reaches the end of the Road and is at rest."

In assessing Asbury's life as an itinerant preacher, it must not be forgotten that he was ill almost continuously throughout his life and seldom without pain. At times he was so weak that he had to be carried out and placed upon his horse, and then when his day's journey had been completed, he had to be lifted from his horse and carried into the house. Scarcely a day passes that he does not make some mention of suffering in his journal. He glories in tribulations. He speaks of sickness as a cross given him to bear. He actually rejoiced in this, for in this way he bore in his body the marks of the dying of the Lord Jesus.

The man without a home had a thousand homes throughout America where, at the fireside, he was ever an honored guest. One night he might be entertained in the elegant house of some general, doctor or politician. The next, he might have to share a room with an entire family, sleeping on a hard chest in the most primitive of conditions. Sometimes he was turned out-of-doors where he found the open sky was his canopy. Sometimes, crippled with rheumatism, he would find temporary shelter under some tree and discover that his companions had lovingly used their own coats to cover him.

"I die daily, am made perfect by labor and suffering, and fill up still what is behind," he tells us. "There is no time or opportunity to take medicine in the day time, I must do it at night. I am wasting away." Then, making his final visit to a home in one of the southern states, he lies down to die in another's bed and in another's home. He has been true to his first resolve: "I have nothing to seek but the glory of God, nothing to fear but His displeasure. I have come to this country with an upright intention, and through the grace of God will make it appear. I am determined that no man shall bias me with soft words and fair speeches; nor will I ever fear the face of man, or know any man after the flesh if I beg my bread from door to door; but whosoever I please or displease, I will be faithful to God, to the people, and to my own soul."

> I would not miss one sigh or tear,
>   Heart-pang, or throbbing brow;
> Sweet was the chastisement severe,
>   And sweet its memory now.
>
> Yes! Let the fragrant scars abide,
>   Love-tokens in Thy stead,
> Faint shadows on the spear-pierced side,
>   And thorn-encompassed head.
>
> —John Henry Newman

45

SAMUEL LOGAN BRENGLE
CALLS BACK

The whole creation groaneth and travaileth
in pain together until now.

ROMANS 8:22

God shall wipe away all tears from their eyes;
and there shall be no more death, neither sorrow, nor crying,
neither shall there be any more pain

REVELATION 21:4

SAMUEL LOGAN BRENGLE, a leading author, teacher and preacher on the doctrine of Holiness, was a commissioner in The Salvation Army. He calls back to us in the following testimony:

"From infancy, my life has been punctuated by tragic losses, surprises and pains. I do not remember my devout father. He made the soldier's supreme sacrifice during the Civil War when I was a very little child, and my earliest recollections are of a bereaved and weeping girl-mother—sighing, sad-faced and broken of heart.

"In my adolescent boyhood when a young fellow most needs his mother, I was away from home at school where I received my first telegram. It read: 'Come home. Come quickly. Mother is dying.' When I reached home my mother, in whose heart I had lived, who had taught me to pray, and had planted deep in my boy-heart the reverent fear of God, lay with folded hands and infinite serenity and peace on her loved face, dead. For the next twelve years I had no home.

"At the beginning of my Salvation Army career, a Boston rough hurled a brick at my head and felled me with a blow that laid me out of the work for eighteen months, and gave me a shock from which I have not wholly recovered in thirty-five years. In the midst of my career, I was stricken down with an agonizingly painful and dangerous sickness in a far-off foreign land, where I lay at death's door among strangers for weary weeks, returning home at last almost helpless, a mere shadow of a man.

"Some years later, lying helpless in a hospital with a great surgical wound that threatened my life, word was brought to me that my sweet wife, the darling of my heart, was dying.

"And now at sixty-four I find myself battered and broken in an automobile accident. The wild excitement of the accident, in spite of the hard blows, seemed to fling me upward on the crest of a great wave, but I soon found myself in the deep trough of a troubled sea of physical depression and pain. I shall not soon forget what a long and painful journey it was from my right side to my left and back again, as I laboriously turned over in bed, and how, to relieve the strained muscles of my neck, I moved my head by pulling my forelock.

"My colleagues and I had been campaigning in the division for five weeks, and between four and five hundred souls had sought pardon and purity. The presence and power of the Holy Spirit were manifest in every place. We were autoing to Grand Rapids for our final week.

"Messages came in from near and far, and in many of these messages were such questions as: 'Why this?' 'Why did it befall you whose hands were so full of useful work? Why did it not fall upon someone who was doing nothing, or who had nothing to do?' 'Was it devil, man, or God that precipitated this upon you?'

"Such questions are natural, but are they asked in wisdom? Every morally earnest and thoughtful person meeting with such an accident will find in the secret of his own heart some answer or answers. One will find it in some moral or spiritual need. He discovers that he had begun to drift, to neglect prayer, to become too much absorbed with things of this life. Paul said he himself was in danger of undue exaltation through the abundance of the revelations given him, therefore God let him be humbled by Satan's thorn. Another may find his answer in a new and needed line of service, in comforting and strengthening other afflicted ones, or in revealing Christ's sufficiency for suffering, as well as service or sacrifice.

"I do not argue, though in fact it may be so, that these are the best things that could have befallen me, but I do testify that by God's grace, by His wise and infinitely loving if mysterious over-ruling, they have all been made to work together for my good, for the enrichment of my own soul and, I trust, of my ministry. They have wrought in me to humble my proud and wayward nature. They have thrown me back on God. They have made me think. They have led to deep searchings of heart in lonely and still hours of the night and to patient and prolonged searchings of the Bible and of history to find out God's ways with men. They have been rigorous and unsparing, but also unfailing, compelling teachers of fortitude, of patience and resignation, of sympathy and understanding. They have drawn out my heart in sympathetic understanding of others. For danger, loss and suffering draw men together and make them conscious that they are bound up in one bundle of life together for weal or woe, while joys and pleasures and abundance separate men into rival groups, contending for mastery and selfish interests, forgetful and indifferent to the welfare of others.

"God may have infinitely bigger purposes than any we imagine. 'I looked for a dewdrop, and found an abyss,' wrote one as he considered the infinite sweep of the plans and purposes of God."

—Samuel Logan Brengle

HELEN FRAZEE BOWER
CALL BACK

The Lord shut him in.
GENESIS 7:16

And God remembered Noah.
GENESIS 8:1

And God blessed Noah
GENESIS 9:1

HELEN FRAZEE BOWER was a very busy mother of five, an author, school teacher, public speaker and Bible teacher. With so many worthy causes making constant demands upon her time, it must have been quite a problem to properly apportion the brief twenty-four hours of each day as was deemed wisest and best. Then, one day in November, 1955, she was struck by a car, crippling her body. Paralyzed, she now had time to learn lessons in stillness and then to pass on those secrets in poetry. In her poem we note that she saw the purpose for the seeming tragedy:

> He said, "Be still"; and I was very still—
> No more a part of all life's fret and rush,
> But laid aside, immobilized, until
> The heavy hours lengthened to a hush
> Of dreary days that closed on emptiness.
> How could the spirit, valiant though it be,
> Exchange the challenges of storm and stress
> For solitude and inactivity?
>
> Then I remembered that He said, "Be still,
> And know that I am God"—and all was changed;
> The knowledge of His presence came to fill
> Each idle moment. I was not estranged
> In some far country, unfamiliar, grim.
> Shut out from things…I was shut in with Him.

ROBERT HALL
CALLS BACK

That I may know him...and the fellowship of his sufferings.
PHILIPPIANS. 3:10

"THE LIFE IS NOT HARDENED and crusted by the hammer of agony, but broken for the escape of its better and more spiritual portion by the buoyant and elastic blows."—P. Brookes.

Robert Hall, the brilliant Baptist pulpit orator, was a chronic sufferer. From his childhood until the close of his ministry, intolerable, gnawing pain interposed upon his pleasure and rest. Hall loved the Gospel message he had been called to proclaim, and though a friendly man, he would often creep away from the merriment of his friends to enjoy communion with his Lord.

His powers of moving people were exceptional. There were times when, to a person, the audience would rise to its feet, and only when his sermon was finished and he had sat down, did they, too, sink down into their seats, not having been aware that they had been standing. Only Hall's intimate acquaintances knew that when his hands quietly gripped his back, he was seeking to alleviate the torturing pain which was incessant even when he was animatedly holding an audience enthralled.

Hall rarely spoke of his complaint to others. His biographer reveals something of the hidden cross this man bore. "There were moments when he could hardly stand on his feet for the merciless gnawing of pain at his body and spirit, but his passion for any high cause and his confidence in the adequacy of spiritual resources never failed to give him the victory.

"At about eleven he usually went to bed, but after two hours' sleep the pain obliged him to leave his bed and seek some sort of rest on the floor or upon an arrangement of three chairs. Then he took up the book he had been reading in the morning."

When about half way through his ministry, the growing intensity of the pain renewed its attack night after night, resulting in a breakdown—physical, mental and nervous. When he had been ordered by the doctor to go the country for quiet and rest, he had filled up the hours of his solitude with incessant reading. Sometimes for twelve hours without a break, he read. Mind and body collapsed, and it was a long, slow pull back to his normal ministry.

Again his biographer says: "Only those few who were in most intimate touch with him, were aware that behind his apparent delight in life and its treasured friendships, there was, as one described it, 'an internal apparatus of torture' which made agony his portion by day and night."

When, after this nervous prostration, he again filled the pulpit, people thronged to hear him. They stood in the aisles; windows were opened to allow those without to listen. But the price this man of God paid for such divine assistance was a 'thorn in the back' which kept him humbly dependent upon God.

The surgeon who performed a post mortem on Hall's body revealed that his life-long agony was due to renal calculus (kidney stones), and gave this tribute to the preacher: "Probably no man ever went through more physical suffering than Mr. Hall: he was a fine example of the triumph of the higher powers of the mind, exalted by religion, over the infirmities of the body." Even when dying, at sixty-seven years of age, he exclaimed, "I have not complained, have I? I will not complain!"

What was the secret of this man's endurance? Robert Hall calls back to us over the years and tells us that he endured by considering the sufferings of Christ. "What are my sufferings to the sufferings of Christ? God has been very merciful. The surest safeguard against complaint or impatience is to contemplate the sufferings of Christ."

"Between the interludes of pain—and pain
　　That made my eyes with sudden tear-drops brim,
I prayed for courage—but I prayed in vain.
　　Then I remembered Him.

"Then I remembered Jesus Christ, Who went
　　The long, long road, alone, to Calvary:
I saw the suffering Savior, stricken, spent—
　　And knew it was for me.

"I thought of all the shamefulness of heart,
　　The human heart, that shrinks from any loss,
From any pain. I felt fresh tear-drops start—
　　But these were for the Cross:

"These were for Him. What selfish tears dare fall,
　　What heart dare say that it has sacrificed?
There is no human suffering at all—
　　When one remembers Christ."

　　　　　　　　　　　　　　—Helen Frazee Bower

ALEXANDER DUFF CALLS BACK

My brethren, count it all joy when ye fall into divers temptations;
Knowing this, that the trying of your faith worketh patience.
But let patience have her perfect work, that ye may be perfect
and entire, wanting nothing.

JAMES 1:2-4

ALEXANDER DUFF, a missionary in India who excelled in Christian education, labored most arduously for the Lord. He was laid aside just when there were the most demands upon him for his ministry. He speaks of this period:

"It so happened that originally the Lord in His gracious providence endowed me with a physical frame that fitted me to encounter almost any amount of labor and fatigue with comparative impunity. But from riding, as it were, on the topmost waves of active exertion, it pleased Him to lay me low, and, flinging me wholly aside, to address me as it were thus: 'You must now for a time, at least, retire from your work a shattered and broken man, and learn to bear your soul in patience before the Lord alone. Sit still away from the world of busy men, and learn the power of solemn silence.'

"And although I must confess that this was hard to bear, with hundreds of doors of usefulness presenting themselves on every side, and that I convulsively struggled against the sentence, yet He soon made me feel that I was in the grasp of an Almighty and invisible power, that held me fast, till I was made to learn the grace of patience and silent, enduring submission to His holy will."

Duff's biographer, George Smith, describes the costly expenditure of physical and nervous energy which his speaking engagements, while on furlough, demanded of him: "On each night, now swaying his arms toward the vast audience around, the tall form kept thousands spellbound and the tardy lights revealed the speaker bathed in the flood of his impassioned appeals. As the thrilling voice died away in the eager whisper which, at the end of his life, marked all his public utterances, and the exhausted speaker fell into a seat, only to be driven home to a couch of suffering, and then of rest barely sufficient to enable his fine constitution to renew and repeat again and again the effort, the observers could realize the expenditure of physical energy which, as it marked all he did, culminated in his prophet-like raptures."

MRS. HOWARD TAYLOR CALLS BACK

The strength of the bearers of burdens is decayed

NEHEMIAH 4:10

A FRIEND WRITING to Mrs. Howard Taylor warns her of too much activity: "How well I understand that nervous breaking down from which you have suffered. Let it be a warning. There is a limit you should not attempt to pass in exhausting labors. It is not easy to fix it, but experience shows pretty clearly where it is. I have been beyond it at times, when all the foundations of life seemed gone. I cannot express what that means, and hope you will never know. Most people have no conception how thin the foundations are which keep them above the abyss, where the interests of life exist no more. I tell you this, for you need to be warned. Learn to say 'No' to invitations or calls to labor which destroy the power to labor and the possibility of service. I do think Howard, as your husband and doctor, should say 'No' for you, and forbid suicidal toils absolutely, firmly, finally. Tell him that with my sincere love."

> "Be still, my child," I heard Him whisper in my ear.
> "'Tis only for a time.
> Tomorrow, out into the raging battle you may go.
> Rest now. Tomorrow you may labor hard and long
> Until at last you will count it a joy to rest.
> But now I ask of thee, 'Be still,'
> And better be prepared for future toil."
>
> —Mary Ann Horst

Doubtless Mrs. Taylor realized that one can do more than God intends him to do. There comes a time in every life when one must

55

learn that one must enter into the rest that remains for all the people of God. God must initiate, empower, direct, if the work is to have lasting consequences. But at seventy-five years of age God still had work for the aged pilgrim to accomplish for Him and she discovered another secret—a supernatural enabling for work done at God's ordering. Mrs. Taylor testifies to it in a letter to a friend.

"I do not know just how, but in the suffering and quietness (enforced) of the past two weeks, He has taken possession afresh of my whole being, so that everything looks different and nothing is difficult any more. I have been, of late, so weary and ineffective. My writing work has been largely at a standstill, and everything has seemed too much for one's strength. I have put it down to growing old (entering one's seventy-fifth year on Christmas Day, you know!), but now I find it is not that at all. It has been—well, just not being filled with the Spirit. But now I see in a new way that the Lord Jesus is willing and able to take the place of self—yes, even at seventy to eighty years of age. Isn't it wonderful? Oh, how glorious and how precious He is! Thank God, there is a Gospel for saints as well as for sinners. Gal. 2:20 never grows old, does it?"

SPURGEON AND MACLAREN CALL BACK

He requested for himself that he might die; and said, It is enough;
now, O Lord, take away my life; for I am not better than my
fathers. ...Then an angel touched him, and said unto him, Arise and
eat. ...And he did eat and drink, and laid him down again.

1 KINGS 19:4-6

WHO WOULD HAVE BELIEVED that Charles Spurgeon, the eloquent
Baptist preacher, who could hold large audiences week after week in
London, would have been so nervously oppressed before entering the
pulpit! Eva Hope writes about the price Spurgeon paid for his public
ministry: "The deacons knew for years he had never entered the pulpit
without such a violent fit of trembling and distress, that sickness often
came upon him. He had often felt as if he would rather be flogged
than face the crowd again.... 'My happy task is one which taxes my
physical, mental and spiritual nature to the uttermost.'"

Out of this affliction, the lesson was learned which he was to pass
on to others: "My witness is that those who are honored of their Lord
in public have usually a secret chastening, or have to carry a peculiar
cross, lest by any means they exalt themselves and fall into the snare
of the devil."

"Dr. Alexander Maclaren," says his biographer, "had a great deal
to overcome before he had control of his nerves; he suffered from what
actors call 'stage fright.' Nerve force inflicts great inconveniences and
sometimes acute pain upon those who have it, but it adds a magnetic
quality to the speech, for the absence of which nothing will compensate.

"When Dr. Maclaren returned to preach at his first church, he
paced the vestry in an agitated way and declared it impossible for a
man of his age to preach twice in one day to the same people with any

possibility of doing good. A few moments later he demonstrated how foolish it would have been for the friends to have excused him from taking the second service."

ELIZABETH FRY
CALLS BACK

O thou afflicted, tossed with tempest, and not comforted,
behold, I will lay thy stones with fair colors, and lay
thy foundations with sapphires.

ISAIAH. 54:11

AS THE GATES of Newgate prison were unlocked, the warders looked on amazed at the composure of Elizabeth Fry, the lone Quakeress, who so fearlessly entered the wards where the women felons were confined, and where the warders would not enter except by twos. Prison officers had warned her that these inmates might claw at her clothes, snatch at any watch or valuable, and even inflict bodily injury. But she dispensed with the usual precautions and gained the confidence and love of these women and small children in order to take the Gospel to them. Later in life, this same Quakeress entered the royal residences of the crowned heads of Europe so that they might consult together about prison reform.

Very few knew, however, that this cultured woman in plain Quakeress dress, who could face the formidable inmates of Newgate, or converse with the crowned heads of Europe, had a nervous disability which at times plunged her into the depths of depression! In the pages of her diary she reveals this trying complaint: "I believe baptisms are necessary for our preparation and refinement for such awful services, in which I desire not to flinch, but to pray that, if consistent with the Divine will, fears may not have dominion over me. In the night I had a deep plunge, making me exceeding low and nervous. The enemy appeared to come in like a flood; I sought after quietness and patience, and in due time, felt a standard to be lifted up against him.

"None know but those who suffer from them, the deep humiliations such disorders create, as those I have lately had. I mean great bodily weakness, accompanied by nervous lowness of spirits, and much mental fear.

"I have known much this winter; the loss of my lovely child—the frequent illnesses in the house amongst the family—loss of property; yet I know hardly any trial, except indeed real evil, that appears so greatly to undermine comfort outwardly and inwardly as a nervous state of body and mind. It calls for watchfulness on the part of those who have it not to give way unduly to it, but I believe few things are really less in our power. It also calls for the most tender compassion and sympathy in others, even if it makes the poor sufferer appear impatient and cross, for it affects the whole frame nearly as much as a bad fever. Indeed, my experience leads me to think that such are attacks of low fever that come under a less conspicuous form than some, and therefore do not attract so much attention. I fully believe that they often occasion greater and more acute internal suffering, than where disease shows itself more distinctly. I think these complaints are, more or less, general, and bring (us) into so much conflict of mind, as well as body, that they should be received as refining trials from the great Head, the Author of all good, and treated such by ourselves and others.

"The less I look outwardly for help, the better, as I do not believe any doctor can do much for me. I feel the best satisfied when I simply endeavor to bear them patiently. They appear to be principally nervous, which I consider beyond the power of man either to understand or cure; but how often have I experienced true spiritual support and help, when I have endeavored patiently to wait on the Source of good, and the mind being so nearly connected with the body, whatever tends to tranquilize it, really helps the complaint."

Elizabeth Fry calls back to tell us that God is the only Source of true help and that whenever He mercifully beckons His busy child aside, it is that he or she might gain new strength in solitude: "I am ready," she comments, "to think that perhaps this state of bodily infirmity is permitted for my mental rest—that I may retire a little from the world and its business."

One Christian speaker and writer, as well as wife and mother, often was severely attacked by most subtle accusations of the devil. Noticing that these attacks usually occurred when she was much wearied through over-exertion, she would take her temperature at these times. She discovered that often the temperature had dropped several degrees below the usual normal reading, and when this happened, instead of endeavoring to spar with the subtle arguments of the evil Accuser, she would relax and rest. Almost always, this brought rest of spirit and relief from the terrible oppression of the enemy.

CHARLES FOX CALLS BACK

I die daily.

1 CORINTHIANS 15:31

I was with you in weakness, and in fear,
and in much trembling.

1 CORINTHIANS 2:3

CHARLES FOX, one of the founders of Keswick and a speaker who had blessed many, experienced the rough hand of the Divine Sculptor in shaping him as a useful vessel. Earlier in his ministry he experienced a time of nervous prostration which necessitated ten years of enforced seclusion. His biographer says of those painful years: "Never a night of whole, unbroken sleep in all those years; never a day without a sense of 'chronic weariness' even in the least suffering times! Was not the upholding grace of God which endows body as well as spirit more manifested thus than in any complete healing!"

The Master knew what He was doing when He called His servant aside. He alone foresaw the fruit that should spring from those precious years of stillness when each battle won was teaching those lessons of death and resurrection with Christ which Fox was later to share so ably with many hungry souls.

Besides his periods of nervous frustration, Charles Fox had an impediment in his speech which, he revealed to his biographer who explains: "It was the only time he ever volunteered to speak of his nervous stammer, which I daresay some of his hearers hardly noticed, and probably none knew how bad it could be. He told me it was worse when a young man. And when he was an applicant for Deacon's orders, the Bishop, after a long interview declined to license him, doing it kindly, but saying that for his own sake it was necessary, as he would never be able to speak in public!

"Young Fox pressed his case. He said he knew what it was, and what he could do; and ultimately, but only after much effort, prevailed. What a moment of importance that was for many thousands in the Church of Christ! He then added that the difficulty came very irregularly, and that sometimes the only way he could manage to find utterance was by throwing out his arms, which seemed to give relief. How few could dream that when, in pulpit or on platform, he was thrilling us with his deep and loving words, he was often fighting a physical battle merely to speak them."

The subject of divine healing was much debated at this time, and Fox's biographer explains his view upon this very important subject: "There is the permanent warp of suffering on which the woof of service is worked. It is only by knowing what his health was, that the full realization of what his service was can be understood. When one of the questions of the last twenty years—that of faith healing—was discussed with him or before him as it often was, he entered closely into it, saying afterwards, 'I know more about it practically than they think I do; they do not know how much I have to practice direct and determined trust in God for the body, and that I could never speak at all if I did not launch myself upon God for the power to do it.'

"He has told how every waking was a miracle of Resurrection, and the undertaking of each new day was like rising up out of death. George Herbert's lines quoted in his last little book, were for years repeated morning by morning, as his constant experience:

> "And now in age I bud again;
> After so many deaths I live and write;
> I once more smell the dew and rain,
> And relish versing: O my light,
>   It cannot be
>   That I am he
> On whom Thy tempests fell at night!"

GEORGE MÜLLER CALLS BACK

His sisters sent unto him, saying,
Lord, behold, he whom thou lovest is sick.

JOHN 11:3

This sickness is not unto death,
but for the glory of God.

JOHN 11:4

GOD DOES NOT CODDLE His loved ones. We find verified this truth verified in the study of Christian biography and experience. We live, however, in an age when many Christians believe that God's purpose is to remove everything painful, everything disappointing, everything to do with poverty and adversity. They declare that God's true servants may expect temporal plenty and an exemption from suffering as an evidence of His blessing. They likewise teach that all forms of illness or distress are from the devil. Often, however, the godliest have been the greatest sufferers.

If ever there was a man in modern times that would seem to deserve divine coddling, it would appear to be George Müller of Bristol. At the very outset of his venture of faith in caring for orphans, he was attacked by a trying form of illness so that he despaired of life for a time. He explains:

"By the mercy of God my head is somewhat relieved. My liver is in a most inactive state, which, as my kind medical attendants tell me, has created the pressure on the top of the head, and through the inactivity of the liver, the whole system having been weakened and my mental exertions having been continued, the nerves of the head have greatly suffered in consequence.

"I have had many distressing moments since I have been at Weston, on account of fearing that my disease may be the forerunner of insanity; yet God has in mercy sustained me. This morning I greatly dishonored the Lord by irritability manifested towards my dear wife, which occurred almost immediately after I had been on my knees before God, praising Him for having given me such a wife....I confessed also my sin of irritability on account of the cold, and sought to have my conscience cleansed through the blood of Jesus. He had mercy, my peace was restored and I sought the Lord again in prayer and had uninterrupted communion with Him."

Before any new enterprise of faith, there is often a corresponding testing of the instrument to be used in this enterprise. This sometimes involves a period of prostration in which the servant of God comes to realize his/her own helplessness. A cholera epidemic had visited Bristol leaving thousands of orphan children whose parents had succumbed to the disease. But George Müller was very disturbed by the general faithlessness of many professed followers of Jesus Christ. He wrote:

"In my visitation of Christians, I found little or no trust in God. I longed to have something I could point a brother to, as a visible proof that God is the same faithful God as ever He was."

One of Müller's co-laborers for years informs us: "On one occasion, after urging fellow-Christians to spend more time in prayer, to exercise more trust in God, and not be anxious for the future, one replied, 'It is all very well for you, sir, but you haven't half-a-dozen children to feed and clothe.' Said Mr. Müller, 'Den I will haf some children and I am sure if God gifs dem to me, He will provide for dem.'"

Müller further explains: "Longing to benefit poor orphans and have them trained in the fear of God, the first and primary object of the work was (and still is) that God might be magnified by the fact that the orphans under my care are provided with all they need only by prayer and faith."

Prior to this liver complaint, George Müller had suffered an illness which had hindered him from walking. He saw God's wonderful hand in curing him of this sickness before this liver affliction struck him. He states: "This was exceedingly kind; for air and exercise are the only means which almost immediately relieve my head. How much greater would have been the affliction, had I not been able to walk about in the air! Truly, 'He stayeth His rough wind, in the day of His east wind.' I delight in pointing out the gentleness of the stroke. I have walked every day for the last thirteen days, between three and four hours a day, and by the mercy of God am able to do so without much fatigue.

"In one other point the Lord has been especially gracious to me in that while I have been unable to preach, unable to write or read much or even to converse for any length of time with the brethren, He has allowed me always sufficient strength for as much secret prayer as I desired. Even praying with others has been often trying to my head; but prayer in secret has not only never tried my head, but has been habitually a relief to my head. How comparatively slight are any trials to a child of God, as long as under them he is enabled to converse freely with his Father. While those favored seasons have lasted, I not only felt the affliction to be no affliction but could call it, from my heart, 'sweet affliction.'

"If it shall ever please the Lord to restore me again, my chief desire is to be sent back to active service with increased humility, greater earnestness in the work, greater love for perishing sinners and a heart habitually influenced by the truths which I preach."

DR. A. T. PIERSON
CALLS BACK

For we would not, brethren, have you ignorant of our trouble which came to us in Asia, that we were pressed out of measure, above strength, insomuch that we despaired even of life.

2 CORINTHIANS 1:8

"WHEN GOD wants to bring more power into your life, He brings more pressure." Many desire more power but not at the cost of more pressure.

> Pressed out of measure and pressed to all length;
> Pressed so intensely, it seems beyond strength;
> Pressed in the body, and pressed in the soul;
> Pressed in the mind, till the dark surges roll.
> Pressure by foes, and pressure by friends—
> Pressure on pressure, till life nearly ends.
>
> Pressed into knowing no helper but God;
> Pressed into loving the staff and the rod.
> Pressed into liberty where nothing clings;
> Pressed into faith for impossible things.
> Pressed into tasting the joy of the Lord;
> Pressed into living a Christlife outpoured.
>
> —Author Unknown

In his book, *The Bible and Spiritual Life,* Mr. Pierson declares: "How many Jacobs are there that cry in sorrow's hour, 'All these things are against me,' while 'all things work together for good!' How many Rachels, bowing over the grave of their little one, refuse to be comforted because they are not! Blessed are they who in the seeming shipwreck of worldly joy and temporal good, cast out of the stern the four blessed anchors of Faith, Hope, Love and Patience, and then, waiting, 'Wish for the day!'

"Lift up your heads, sorrowing saints! Glory in tribulations, for it worketh patience, and patience experience, and what is experience? It is the approval of God: the stamp of the Divine Assayer 'approved.' When the Lord rejects the metal, he stamps it 'reprobate'; when He releases it from the alloy so that it mirrors His own face, He stamps it 'approved!'"

Dr. Pierson, who had except for minor illnesses kept up a very steady life of spiritual activity, experienced two serious bouts of illness when in his sixtieth year. In January he was suddenly attacked by a very severe pain which proved to be inflammation of the bladder. He suffered six months of the most intensive and constant pain. The doctors endeavored in vain to bring relief, and more than one physician warned him that his life of public service was over. But his Heavenly Father had other views and purposes in what was happening. What appeared to the observer to be a sudden termination of usefulness was in reality the application of pressure which was to greatly multiply his spiritual power and efficacy. Observers knew neither the "patient nor the plans of the patient's God."

He was visited by a second affliction toward the end of the year. His head and ears began to trouble him so as to interfere with his hearing and made continuous mental exertion difficult. The conviction that God was his physician had become stronger as he had associated with George Müller, whom he considered both a prophet and patriarch, and who had most influenced his life.

His biographer speaks of the course of action Mr. Pierson took: "He consulted a physician who said he evidently had inflammation of the inner ear, and advised him at once to consult an aurist. On five or six occasions his suffering was so severe that he started to consult a specialist, but stopped and turned back before reaching the door. He had many warm friends among the physicians and greatly honored them and their profession, so that he did not on ordinary occasions refuse the use of medicine, but at this time it seemed to him that God was testing his faith. He determined to leave his case in the hands of God and exactly one month later, all trouble disappeared.

"Upon a second examination the same physician found his ears in a perfectly normal condition. The trouble never returned. This was Dr. Pierson's first marked experience of divine healing and he came more and more to depend upon God to give him physical strength. His great emphasis was on man's duty to submit body, mind and spirit entirely to God and study the laws relating to physical and spiritual health."

"I say to you," said Dr. Pierson, "with the solemnity of a dying man, that no man has ever yet laid hold on the supernatural power of God as it is possible to lay hold on that power. God's great plan for human life is that the Holy Spirit, entering into man's spirit, shall transform man's convictions, his emotions, his sensibilities, his resolutions and even his body....I do not say that all disease is a result of sin, but I am bold to say that we know very little of what the power of God means in transforming disposition and intellect and conduct. We have still less conception of what blessing might come even to the bodies of the saints, if the Apostolic faith, Apostolic power return to the Church."

The last twelve years were the most fruitful of Mr. Pierson's entire life. God's words to St. Paul were fulfilled in this servant: "My strength is made perfect in weakness." God's choice of weak things to confound the mighty was proving that the apparently feeble tool, handed to God unreservedly, performed wonders in Christ's kingdom.

PAIN-RACKED
INTERCESSORS CALL BACK

I remember thee upon my bed,
and meditate on thee in the night watches.

PSALMS 63:6

In the night his song shall be with me,
and my prayer unto the God of my life.

PSALMS 42:8

"A LIFE FILLED with pain is perhaps meant to be a life filled with prayer."—Dora Greenwell

"Let sorrow be converted into prayer."—Bishop Westcott

"How wonderful the children of pain have taken honors in the school of prayer! Sufferers have oftentimes been transcendent intercessors. Crowd your life, your pained life, my much afflicted friend, with the prayer which is the best service of humanity, and with the worship of the heart which is the sacrifice God loves best."—Anon.

Mr. Moody and Mr. Sankey had an invitation to go to Cambridge to preach but they were loath to go for, as Moody said, "I have no call to go to universities." But eventually they did go, and disturbance at first so marred the meeting that Moody wondered if fifty had heard Mr. Sankey's songs. Then things changed, and Moody reveals the reason:

"A lady, a bed-ridden saint, who was very interested in the work, sent around word to a few Christians to get together in a little upper-room to plead with God for a change in these students. That turned the tide. It wasn't the preaching. They had heard better sermons in the Church of England by some of the best preachers. It was those Christians in that upper-room, praying to God that made the difference.

And how they did pray! It seemed as if their prayers burst into Heaven and I said, 'The victory is ours.' There was a hush over the audience and fifty-two men sprang to their feet and went up into the gallery, and we had all the enquirers we could deal with."

At another time, Mr. Moody again felt great power attending his service and knew that there was a secret somewhere. He later discovered that an invalid by the name of Marion Adlard had set herself to fasting and praying in her bedroom for Mr. Moody. The result was outstanding.

Mr. Finney was also indebted to those sick and weak in body, who sent petitions to Heaven on his behalf. Of one he said, "Soon after I first saw Rev. Daniel Nash, he was confined to his room with disease of his eyes, and was almost entirely blind about six months. During this period he gave himself to much prayer, and had a great searching and overhauling in his spiritual life, and, before he could see enough to be abroad, was powerfully baptized with the Holy Ghost.

"I wrote asking him to join me in keeping every Friday as a day of fasting and prayer for the more general out-pouring of the Holy Spirit. He replied that his body was nearly worn out, that the Holy Spirit had laid the world upon his heart and pressed him almost to death. Those who knew him, during the period of which I speak, will never forget his prayers, and the unutterable groanings with which he was exercised by the Holy Spirit.

"The spirit of prayer that was upon him was quite a stumbling block to professors of religion who had never known the Holy Ghost as the Spirit that maketh intercession for the saints according to the will of God with groanings which cannot be uttered.

"He was a most wonderful man in prayer, one of the most earnest, devout, spiritually-minded, heavenly-minded men I ever saw. He labored about in many places in central and northern New York, and gave himself up to almost constant prayer, literally praying himself to death at last. He was found dead in his room in the attitude of prayer."

Rev. C. F. Cushman relates another similar incident: "An unaccountable revival broke out in a congregation in a village, and about one hundred were converted in a few weeks. At last, a minister discovered the secret of the revival and relates it thus: 'There is a sister in my church who has for years been an invalid, and confined to her bed. I rode out to see her. As I sat by her bedside she said, "You have had a very precious revival." "We have," I answered. "I knew it was coming," she said. And then she proceeded to give her pastor an account of the burden that had been upon her for weeks, and the manner in which her soul had gone out in prayer for the unconverted, in midnight hours and at other times. Before the interview closed, the pastor felt that the unaccountable revival was accounted for.'"

Yes, I would have chosen my life to be
　　Active, tireless and strong;
A constant, ceaseless working for Him
　　Amid the needy throng.

But He chose for me a better lot,
　　A life of frequent pain,
Of strength withheld when 'twas needed most,
　　And loss instead of gain.

He gave me work of another kind,
　　Far, far above my thought,
The work of interceding with Him
　　For souls that He had bought.

—Unknown

Is any among you afflicted? let him pray (Jas. 5:13).

BOOK 2
LONELINESS

GOD'S STURDY TREES
CALL BACK

"To appoint unto them that mourn in Zion, to give unto them beauty
for ashes, the oil of joy for mourning, the garment of praise for the
spirit of heaviness; that they might be called trees of righteousness,
the planting of the Lord, that he might be glorified"

ISAIAH 61:3

"THE REASON there is so much shallow living, so much talk but little obedience, is that so few are prepared to be like the pine on the hilltop—alone in the wind for God, where are shaken loose from us the things that can be shaken, that those things which cannot be shaken may remain. We who follow the Crucified are not here to make a pleasant thing of life; we are called to suffering for the sake of a suffering, sinful world.

"His brow was crowned with thorns; do we seek rosebuds for our crowning?

"His hands were pierced with nails; are our hands ringed with jewels?

"His feet were bare and bound; do our feet walk delicately?

"What do we know of travail?—of tears that scald before they fall?—of heartbreak?—of being scorned?

"God forgive us that so often we turn our faces from a life that is even remotely like His, enjoying our possessions on earth. 'Whosoever doth not bear his cross and come after me cannot be my disciple.'"—Amy Carmichael

> "Lord, let me learn from an old tree
> That there is dignity in loneliness,
> Beauty in broken branches,
> Strength in twisted, storm-beaten torso.

Help me to understand that underneath—
If roots go deep enough—
No storm can wreck the life
That from them reaches to the sky."

—Unknown

To expect to have the strength of an oak without enduring the storms of life is an impossibility. As Horace Bushnell puts it:

"If the oak cannot be rooted firmly without heavy storms, why should we ask to be made strong in feeble resistance and small conquests? What is a creature on trial for a character but a candidate for temptations, a necessary subject of temptations? We have never one too many or too strong, unless we make them artificially so by yielding when we ought to resist. Great temptations are great battles. Just there it is that God most honors us—by calling us to be heroes and waiting with us on the field to crown us."

Thank God for those wind-swept heroes who faced the fierce storms of the mountain-top. How else could the fine grain of their Christian character have been produced? Like the "trees" in the following story, they are set apart for special uses and choice service.

"A traveler was in Italy when one day he stood watching a lumberman, who, as the logs floated down the swift mountain stream, occasionally jabbed his hook into one and drew it carefully aside. He said to the man, 'Why do you pick out these few, for they all look alike?'

"The lumberman replied, 'They all look alike, but they are not all alike, Signor. The logs I let pass are grown in the valley where they have been protected all their lives. Their grain is coarse; they are good only for lumber. But, these logs, Signor, grew on the mountains. From the time they were sprouts and saplings they were lashed and buffeted by the winds, and so they grew strong with fine grain. We save them for choice work; they are not lumber, Signor.'

"Has not God chosen souls for choice work, but how often does the enemy try to thwart that plan of God!"—Sel.

> Good timber does not grow in ease.
> The stronger the wind, the tougher the trees.
> The farther the sky, the greater the length.
> The more the storm, the more the strength.
> By rain and cold, by wind and snow
> In tree or man, good timber grow.
>
> Where thickest stand the forest growth
> We find the Patriarch of both.
> And they hold converse with the stars,
> Whose broken branches show the scars
> Of many winds and much of strife.
> This is the Common Law of Life.
>
> Spiritual men are born in strife,
> Their goal is set—eternal life!
> Their feet are rooted deep in prayer,
> All their possessions are "over there."
> Fire-charred, storm-wracked and twisted here,
> They live because of One held dear.
>
> And like the tree which storms did tear
> While lightning slashed the icy air;
> They keep their eyes upon the stars
> And glory in their blood and scars,
> Knowing full well when storms have passed,
> They'll stand, sun crowned, victor at last.
>
> —Unknown

ALPINE CLIMBERS CALL BACK

"...He went up into a mountain apart to pray: and when the evening was come, he was there alone."

MATTHEW 14:23

"**P**EOPLED AND WARM is the valley, lonely and chill the height," wrote the poet. The aspiring Christian, longing for more, will begin to find himself less understood the farther up he climbs. "If we are bent on being more spiritual, we can afford to walk pretty much alone."

There is plenty of company among professed followers of Christ, sunning themselves among others in the protected and congenial spiritual valleys of Christian worship. Now and again, however, there have always been the few who determine to ascend the mounts with God in their search for deeper truths. The ranks soon thin out as the climber reaches the more rugged slopes of the higher altitudes. The views of breath-taking splendor cannot be shared with the valley dweller who is incapable of participation in the widened horizons of the climber.

Charles Spurgeon lamented the lonely road: "No-one knows, but he who has endured it, the solitude of a soul that has outstripped its fellows in zeal for the Lord of hosts. It does not reveal itself, lest men count it madness; it cannot conceal itself, for the fire burns within its bones; only before the Lord does it find rest."

Someone has said, "The road to achievement is a very lonesome trail, but the lonesome trail has one great advantage—few get in our way."

George Müller wrote: "He who will fly as an eagle, which goes into the higher levels where cloudless day abides and lives in the sunshine of God, must consent to live a comparatively lonely life. No

78

bird is as solitary as the eagle. Eagles never fly in flocks; one, or at the most two, are ever seen at once. But the life that is lived unto God, however it forfeits human companionship, knows divine fellowship. And the child of God, who, like his Master, undertakes to 'do always those things that please him,' can, like his Master say: 'The Father hath not left me alone. I am alone, yet not alone, for the Father is with me.'"

Another famous Alpine climber shares with us her pangs of loneliness when she found so few with whom to share her inmost convictions. Listen to Catherine Booth, who, while still very young, opens up her heart to William Booth:

"You will not understand me when I say that I never yet met with a female friend able to understand or appreciate my views and feelings on the great subjects which appear to me the only realities of life. All whom I know seem to live in a different world. They look not at the future; they seem to be shut up in the present little paltry things of everyday life. I am grieved that it is so; the mothers of humanity want different training."

Later in a sermon she preached on "Charity and Loneliness" she further explains: "The possession of this Divine Charity often necessitates walking in a lonely path. Not merely in opposition and persecution, but alone in it. And here again, Jesus, Who was the personification of divine love, stands out as our great example. He was emphatically alone, and of the people there was none with Him. Even the disciples whom He had drawn nearest to Him, and to whom He had tried to communicate most of His thought and spirit, were so behind that He often had to reprove them, and to lament their obtuseness and want of sympathy: 'Ye shall leave me alone.' In the greatness of His love, He had to go forward into the darkness of Gethsemane. He was alone while they slept, and then He went all alone, through ribaldry, scorn and sarcasm, to the Judgment Hall. He stood alone before Pilate. On the cross He hung unaccompanied! Alone!

"And as it was with the Master, so it has been with all those whom God has called to go in advance of their race. It was so with Paul, 'At my first answer no man stood with me'; and it has commonly been so with those whom God has called to extraordinary paths. Must John have a revelation of things shortly to come to pass? He must go alone into the Isle of Patmos. Must Paul hear unspeakable words, not, at that time, lawful for a man to utter? He must go alone into the third heaven, and not be allowed even to communicate what he saw and heard when he came down. In advance of other saints, he must necessarily go alone.

"And just so, when God has called some of His followers to an out-of-the-way path, they have had to go alone in an untrodden way. Superior love necessitates a lonely walk. I wish I could make it easier, but I cannot help it. I simply state the fact, that superior love necessitates, in some measure, a lonely walk, because, you see, it is only they who thus love to whom the Lord tells His secrets. If you want to ask a confidential question and get a confidential answer, you must be on the bosom of your Master. You won't be able to do it at a distance. Then, you see, when He gives to any soul superior light to its fellows and that soul follows the light, it necessarily entails a path in advance of its fellows. Unless He can inspire and encourage them to follow, which alas is hard work, he must go on alone."

> Holy in voice and heart,
>   To high ends, set apart!
> All unmated! All unmated!
> Just because so consecrated!
>
> Vaunting to come before
>   Our own age evermore!
> In a loneness, in a loneness,
> And the nobler for that oneness!

But if alone we be,—
  Where is our empery?
And if none can reach our stature,
Who can meet our lofty nature?

—E. B. Browning

FAITH'S HEROINES CALL BACK

"I watch, and am as a sparrow alone upon the house top."

PSALMS 102:7

"LONELINESS is the Christian worker's greatest enemy," wrote Lela McConnell, an intrepid adventurer for God in the Kentucky Mountains and founder of the K. M. H. A. (Kentucky Mountain Holiness Association). "It is the open door to Satan's most vicious attacks. Temptations that make little or no appeal under normal conditions become almost irresistible in times of solitude. Hardships, persecutions, poverty, work and all else that the missionary has to face, fades into insignificance in comparison to life alone. The memory of dear ones left behind, bosom friends far away, days and nights of utter solitude and loneliness—it is this that is hardest to bear. No one to talk to, no one to pray with—I mean, no one who sympathizes and understands.

"It was just such an experience that caused me, when I was stationed among the mountaineers of Kentucky and had to live in a cottage alone, to express my feelings in the following lines:

> 'Lonely! Lonely! Lonely!
>   In the heart of the mighty hills
> And I sigh for the dear, home faces,
>   And fancy a thousand ills.
>
> 'A dog! A friend! A loved one!
>   Or anything that has life;'
> But I wait in vain for an answer
>   And alone I face the strife.

'The work, the care, the struggle,
　I greet with thankful heart;
But to be alone in the mountain
　That is the hardest part.

'Lonely! Lonely! Lonely!
　In the light of the waning moon;
Dear God in Heaven, have mercy
　And send a friend to me soon!'"

—USED BY PERMISSION
of K.M.H.A.

Then there is the solitude of the city as well as that of the mountains: "The spirit of unrelatedness in towns is no new thing. Francis Bacon, writing in 1607, refers to this problem: 'A crowd,' he says, 'is not company, and faces are but a gallery of pictures, and talk but a tinkling cymbal where there is no love.' He goes on to quote a Latin proverb which shows that in Roman times men knew that the greater the city, the greater could be one's loneliness in the midst of it."

Emma Booth was matron of the Salvation Army Training Home in London. She describes in a letter the pangs of loneliness which she experienced in that metropolis: "I was thinking last night, it was not the thorn or spear which made Calvary hardest to bear. It must have been the keen sense of loneliness which made the cup the bitterest. And yet, we know He was not alone.

"Of course, I know my own heart too well not to understand that this is my weak spot. Ten thousand times it is easier to go in and doubt and fear on this spot than on any other; and lately there has been a big, huge battle to fight, unseen in its full sense by any but God. I have felt I must have something, big, intense, to love back again, if I had to take one of London's mongrel terriers to my bosom—something true and good and safe, and just of my own, loving me with all the love of an affectionate heart. But I see that has been denied me. God knows perhaps it would be best, and I see I must embrace, not only what is good, but what is best. So much hangs on our going all lengths. Even though some steps we take in darkness may never be seen by others till we stand in the light together, they will be seen then. Oh, yes, I must be brave. I will be, I will be!

"For me henceforth to live shall be Christ, and I must faster learn to know no man or woman after the flesh. Even my heart God is able to deliver and keep! Oh! I have suffered so, so much. I am like a weary traveler, who is tired, and has found no rest; and now I will seek no more but to His dear arms at last I'll fly, there only."

"He came to the desert of London Town
    Grey miles long;
He wander'd up and he wander'd down
    Singing a quiet song.

"He came to the desert of London Town,
    Mirk miles broad;
He wandered up and he wandered down
    Ever alone with God.

"There were thousands and thousands of human kind
    In this desert of brick and stone
But some were dead and some were blind,
    And he was there alone."

—William Blake

George Bowen never married and never had a furlough during his forty years of service in India. He doubtless knew much of temptations to loneliness, but he found how to triumph over desolation. He says:

"Sometimes, the most bitter experience of desolation is in the crowded walks of men, sometimes in the bosom of a large family.

Nothing is more desolating than to be closely surrounded on every side by those who are called friends, kinsfolk, but who have no manner of sympathy with the ruling sentiment of our heart. Often has one so situated longed for the most lonely spot, and deeply felt that the solitary place would be glad, beautiful, heaven-like in comparison with his situation.

"But often again has such a soul turned to God and found it possible to obtain a triumph over its desolation. The Life of God perfected in that soul has sent forth streams into the uncongenial elements around, and so vindicated itself by celestial love and patience that they too have been led to drink and live. How blessed a thing was it that that soul could not escape in the day of its weariness!"

GOD'S TRAVELERS CALL BACK

"And every man went unto his own house.
Jesus went unto the Mount of Olives"

JOHN 7:53, 8:1

G. H. LANG traveled extensively all over the world preaching, counseling and praying. In his book, *An Ordered Life*, he shares with his readers a brief and unusual encounter he had with "loneliness."

"Temptation approaches from many directions. Week after week alone is not good for any man. On Sunday morning, I spoke at the meeting of the American Mission then held in a shop. Several thanked me warmly, but not one of them asked if I would return home and lunch with them. I felt neglected as I returned to my large and silent flat. It was foolish; perhaps not one of them knew of my circumstances—Americans are usually most hospitable. But I thought of the words, 'They went every man to his own house. Jesus went to the Mount of Olives.' That afternoon the ever-present Lord the more endeared Himself to my heart, and I wrote the lines:

"The men He had made to their homes repaired,
　　To their homes with their joys and pleasures;
But the Man Who had made them, a Stranger here,
　　Possessed neither home nor treasures;
The Pharisee turned to his lordly house,
　　To his loaded board and his cushioned bed,
While the Teacher went to the lonely mount,
　　On the bare, cold earth to lay down His head.

"The languid lawyer was lulled to sleep
　　By the plaintive pipe and the rhythmic song;
Nor a moment was kept from his slumber deep
　　By the orphan's wail or the widow's wrong;

But the only music the Savior heard
    Was the wind as it rustled the olive trees;
And few were the hours that He spent in sleep,
    And many He passed on bended knees.

"The cold night air chilled His weary frame,
    But His spirit rose undaunted;
For to share the sorrows of men He came,
    By His Father's will appointed:
And the whole of the burden He needs must bear
    Of the poor and despised and neglected;
And so that the Helper of all He may be,
    He, though Lord of all, is rejected.

"Ah, lowly Savior, I choose with Thee
    Thy portion so satisfying;
To be scorned of the world that knows not God,
    To share both Thy life and Thy dying:
Far better to walk with Thee and weep,
    Than to laugh with the godless worldling,
For Thou art Thyself my boundless joy,
    When my soul is Thy company sharing.

"And who that has watched on the mount with Thee
    Will crave for a night of pleasure?
Or who that has tasted Thy love most sweet
    Will leave it for other treasure?
My choice is to share Thy toil and pain,
    Thou lonely but lovely Savior;
Accounting Thy cross my richest gain,
    To win Thine eternal favor.

"To know e'en now Thine entrancing bliss
    Of helping the weary-hearted;
Till the guilty soul shall praise Thy name
    For the dread of doom departed:

To know at last Thine eternal joy,
    And to share Thy heavenly glory—
This, this is my choice, Thou despised of men,
    And Thyself my unchanging story."

—G. H. Lang, 1959 ©The Paternoster Press
USED BY PERMISSION

"When the late Dr. Henry C. Morrison came home from one of his many travels, we are told that he arrived in the City of New York at the same time and on the same ship that brought the great 'Teddy' Roosevelt from one of his hunting trips to Africa. Literally thousands swarmed the docks to greet the noted hunter, but not a soul was there to welcome Dr. Morrison. Dr. Morrison relates how Satan, the accuser, whispered to him, 'Aha, see how they greet the men of the world, and you—one of God's preachers—without a single soul to greet you!' This man of God admitted that in the loneliness of his heart, there could have been place for a hurt, but the Father sweetly whispered, 'Yes, but Henry, you are not home yet.'"—Selected

Alone! Yes, Jesus was alone
In that great stretch of sand and stone,
And later in earth's noise and din—
Alone, since He was free from sin.
And men who gathered to be taught,
Oft failed to reach His inmost thought;
Still later 'neath a darkened sky,
They listened to a lonely cry
From One upon th' accursed tree:
"O, why hast Thou forsaken Me?"
We pause, and pray, "Lord help us guess
The depth of that great loneliness."

—E. E. Trusted

DAVID HILL
CALLS BACK

"I have been an alien in a strange land."

EXODUS 2:22

THERE IS ANOTHER form of loneliness which is most poignant because it comes as a result of our choice when we answer the call of God. We leave friends and relatives for a people of a strange speech and a hard language. We exchange a structure of civilization familiar to us, for unaccustomed codes and rules of an alien environment.

This strange transition was felt by Bishop Selwyn when, as a young man, he went out as a missionary to New Zealand. One can almost feel the oppression of unutterable loneliness he experienced in this diary entry: "A great change has taken place in the circumstances of my natural life, but the change need not affect my spiritual life. Here is a land where not so much as a tree resembles those of my native country. All visible things are new and strange, but the things which are unseen remain the same."

David Hill, and English missionary sent out by the Methodists to China, was gripped by this same sense of loneliness. As a pioneer, he sacrificed marriage because he felt he could ask no beloved partner to face alone the many days and weeks which his constant itineration would necessitate. Although possessed of ample means, he lived a life of extreme simplicity, while lavishly bestowing upon other missionary couples those very things which he had denied himself.

He shared his moments of heart loneliness with his relatives through letters and diary:

"There are times in a missionary's life when the sense of loneliness, the keen want of human sympathy, cuts home like a bleak and bitter east wind. And to learn to stand alone in any course of action, duty, or suffering without one word of human sympathy, is a great lesson to learn ....

"You can't tell how it awakens one's sympathies to look at the faces of old friends, real friends, loved friends. As I sit here all alone with these hundreds of Chinamen all around, who every time we go out call us the worst names they can, whose very dogs (of which nearly every house has one) bark with such incessant roar as we walk some of the streets, and then realize that you can number on your fingers all of them whose feeling towards you reaches anything near to love,—as these thoughts come over one, and they do sometimes, it does one good to recall old faces, and especially such faces ....

"In the great inward struggles of a man's life he is almost always, as far as I have seen, intensely alone. This indeed constitutes the terribleness of the struggle. No one can go with him; God intended that he should be isolated from all his fellows and work out the problem alone. And hence it is not from unkindness but from actual inability to sympathize with such a struggle that friends can give no, or very little, aid, but He can, Who 'was tempted in all points like as we are....'"

David Hill had evidently discovered the treasures of darkness and loneliness—an intimate relationship with God. These treasures shine forth through an extract from a letter to his father: "'Son, thou art ever *with Me*' indicates the real fountain-spring of satisfaction. Trench says that many misread this verse, placing the emphasis on *ever* whereas it should be on the *with Me*. 'Thou are ever *with Me*,' and what more canst thou desire? Can fatted calves or finger-rings compare with thy being *with Me*?"

> There is a mystery in human hearts,
> And though we be encircled by a host
> Of those who love us well, and are beloved,
> To every one of us, from time to time,
> There comes a sense of utter loneliness.

Our dearest friend is "stranger" to our joy,
And cannot realize our loneliness.
"There is not one who really understands,
Not one to enter into all I feel";
Such is the cry of each of us in turn.

We wander in a "solitary way,"
No matter what or where our lot may be;
Each heart, mysterious even to itself,
Must live its inner life in solitude.
And would you know the reason why this is?

It is because the Lord desires our love
In every heart He wishes to be first.
He therefore keeps the secret-key Himself,
To open all its chambers, and to bless
With perfect sympathy, and holy peace,
Each solitary soul who comes to Him.

So when we feel this loneliness, it is
The voice of JESUS saying, "Come to Me":
And every time we are "not understood,"
It is a call to us to come again;
For Christ alone can satisfy the soul,
And those who walk with Him from day to day
Can never have "a solitary way."

And when beneath some heavy cross you faint,
And say, "I cannot bear this load alone,"
You say the truth. Christ made it purposely
So heavy that you must return to Him.

The bitter grief, which "no one understands,"
Conveys a secret message from the King,
Entreating you to come to Him again.
The Man of Sorrows understands it well,
In all points tempted, HE can feel with you.

—A. C.

MISSIONARY PIONEERS CALL BACK

"Ye shall be scattered, every man to his own, and shall leave me alone: and yet I am not alone, because the Father is with me"

JOHN 16:32

IN THE BOOK, *The Best of J. H. Jowett*, we have from his pen a most touching sketch of the brave pioneer missionary to Mongolia:

"I think of James Gilmour. I think of the wild, far-stretching field to which he addressed his uncompanioned life. Consider the size of the field. Mongolia stretches from the Sea of Japan on the east to Turkestan on the west, a distance of three thousand miles, and from the southern boundary of Asiatic Russia to the Great Wall of China, a distance of nine hundred miles. Into that mighty field put down a single man and let him attempt single-handed the heavy work of evangelizing it for Christ. Again, I say, 'What a field!' And again I say, 'What a ploughman!'

"I greatly like that first entry in his diary when he had just got his share in the uncut field: 'Astir by daybreak. Made porridge and tea.' (How like John Tauler, the mystic, in its combination of homely duty and sublime task!). 'Made porridge and tea. Several huts in sight. Oh, let me live for Christ, and feel day by day the blessedness of a will given up to God.'

"And so he ploughed away, and in unthinkable loneliness. 'My eyes have filled with tears frequently these last few days in spite of myself! Oh, the intense loneliness of Christ's life! He bore it! O Jesus, let me follow in Thy steps.'

"In after days was there much to cheer him in the furrow he had cut? 'In the shape of converts I have seen no results. I have not, as far as I am aware, seen anyone who even wanted to be a Christian.' He writes again: 'Oh, if things would only move.' How then? Did he turn back? Oh, no, he never looked back! He found his sufficiency in his Savior, and he died in the furrow.

"In one of his last letters to his brother he wrote, 'In Jesus is all fullness. Supply yourself from Him. Heaven's ahead, brother, Hurrah!' I know of no more heartening word in missionary literature than this 'Hurrah!' from this much worn ploughman, cutting his day's furrow in the tremendous field of Mongolia."

> Is there a secret path of life
>   Which you must tread alone?
> A coastguard walk, with danger rife,
>   A walk which must be done?
> You think it is a narrow way
>   And only room for you—
> Your Father is just there today
>   For there is room for two.
>
> Is there a secret cave of grief,
>   A dark and dreary place?
> Are you cut off beyond relief,
>   Where wild sea waves embrace?
> You think you are alone, sad child,
>   That none can come to you;
> But in that cavern lone and wild,
>   There always will be two.
>
> Are you in secrets none may know,
>   Alone upon the sea,
> Where unknown winds around you blow,
>   Tempted as none may be?
> Your Father is upon the deck.
>   Alone? It is not true:
> Though battered, beaten, half a wreck,
>   The lone boat still holds two.

Dear child, there is no secret place
　　Of work, or want, or woe,
But what your Father's smiling face
　　Is there. You cannot go
Unto the closet of your life,
　　But it will still be true:
When most alone, 'mid calm or strife,
　　There always will be two.

　　　　　　　　　　　—W. L.

Hudson Taylor, another young, lone ambassador for Christ in one of the most populated lands in the world, pours out his heart in a letter to his mother after having been robbed of all: "I sometimes wonder if I shall ever be settled, and long for a fixed and permanent position and a partner to share in all my joys and sorrows, labors and encouragements. But the only true rest is in following Jesus whithersoever He goes; the only true repose is in laboring for Him. And while I long for quiet, even now, after a week of it, I long to be at work again, speaking of Jesus' love.

"At home you can never know what it is to be alone—absolutely alone, without one friend, with everyone looking on you with curiosity, with contempt, with suspicion or with dislike. Thus to learn what it is to be despised and rejected of men, thus to learn what it is to have nowhere to lay your head, and then to have the love of Jesus applied to your heart by the Holy Spirit—His holy, self-denying love—this is worth coming for. Oh to know more of Him, and the power of His resurrection, and the fellowship of His sufferings, being made conformable unto His death! The flesh would say, 'Use not this prayer, you know not what you ask';—but 'God is love.'"

SAMUEL BRENGLE
CALLS BACK

"All they which are in Asia be turned away from me."

2 TIMOTHY 1:15

"At my first answer no man stood with me, but all men forsook me: I pray God that it may not be laid to their charge. Notwithstanding the Lord stood with me, and strengthened me."

2 TIMOTHY 4:16-17

IN THE MIDST of my Army career, I was stricken down with an agonizingly painful and dangerous sickness in a far-off foreign land, where I lay at death's door among strangers for weary weeks, returning home at last almost helpless, a mere shadow of a man. Some years later, lying helpless on a hospital bed, with a great surgical wound that threatened my life, word was brought to me that my sweet wife, the darling of my heart, was dying....

Oh, it is easy to preach in full and robust health about grace, fathomless as the sea; grace enough for me, but the test comes in proving and practicing it in danger, in broken health, in poverty, in loneliness and neglect, in sore trial;

> The toad beneath the harrow knows
> Precisely where each sharp tooth goes;
> The butterfly along the road
> Preaches contentment to the toad.

The rub will come to the butterfly when he too gets under the harrow. Can he preach contentment then? I would not like to go through life without some hard blows when so many of my fellow-men must suffer them, and when my Master was a "Man of sorrows, and acquainted with grief," wounded and bruised. If I am to understand

Him and my fellow-men I must share in the common experience of life. If I am to have inside knowledge of His power and willingness to help and sustain, I must have inside experiences that call for His help. A manifold testimony with power demands a firsthand knowledge of manifold mercies. The value of testimony depends upon the degree and certainty of knowledge....

Poor? I have known dire poverty, been without a dollar, but He clothed and fed me. He said He would, and He did.

Lonely? I have wandered with aching heart through the dark labyrinthine dungeons of loneliness, and I found Him there, and was no more lonely....

Fearful? Afraid? I have known nights of torturing fear, and then He has drawn nigh and said, "It is I; be not afraid" (Matt. 14:27), and all my fears have fled away, and I wondered at the fullness of my peace and calm.

Pain? Agony? I have been wracked and tortured till it seemed I could bear no more, and then I remembered His pain and agony for me on Golgotha, and my spirit bowed in adoration and rose up in exultation that I should be permitted to know something of His physical agony, and then I welcomed pain with a shout of solemn, triumphant joy. My pain seemed to fade away, and I forgot it in the fullness of my peace, my joy, my fellowship with Him.

—S. L. Brengle

Talk not of strength, till your heart has known
And fought with weakness through long hours alone.

Talk not of virtue, till your conquering soul
Has met temptation and gained full control.

Boast not of garments, all unscorched by sin,
Till you have passed unscathed through fires within.

—Author unknown

C. T. STUDD
CALLS BACK

"...For I called him alone, and blessed him, and increased him."

ISAIAH 51:2B

PIONEERS who have launched out at God's command into some new territory have never done so without confronting almost insurmountable difficulties. The Prince of this world does not yield easily the territory which he has held for centuries. He will fiercely contend for every inch of ground gained by these Gospel invaders. Contrary to the popular opinion that God promises immunity from difficulties, we find just the opposite. The price in loneliness, disappointments, frustrations and financial shortages, is what such intrepid pioneers have had to pay.

C. T. Studd opened up a territory for God in the heart of Africa and was no exception or favorite. If weakness is what God chooses in His instruments, then Studd majored in this qualification. He was already in his fifties. Instead of possessing a robust constitution with which to encounter and overcome the obstacles which such a venture would demand, he had seven different physical diseases warring within his tall, spare frame. No doctor would grant him a permit for such a "fool's" attempt.

Loneliness? Yes, Studd knew many long, long years of separation from his partner in life. He had only been on the field a brief time when word came that she was dangerously ill. What would he do? Retire from the field? We will let him tell the story contained in the book he wrote entitled, *Reminiscences of Mrs. C. T. Studd by Her Husband:*

"The mail of one week brought the news of the death of our President and our Chairman. I have never been able to arrive at the proper calculation as to which exceeded: our loss or our honor. The loss of two such men was very great as anyone who knew them would know, but then the honor that God should specially invite two chief members of our Mission—such a small mission,—too—was a very extraordinary honor. Of course, when God removes two such worthy men He only does so because He is going to occupy the place Himself. And then there was a very great honor to ourselves for it was evident that God had considerable confidence in us, knowing that we should not falter even though so great a blow struck us.

"And yet even this was not the first great calamity that came upon us. A calamity? No! Only another trial of our faith. My wife became terribly ill. The doctor on examination said she could not possibly live. Lord Radstock prayed for her and she did not die. Then the doctors said that she must be an invalid for the rest of her life, and that I must be ordered home. I have not the faintest doubt that the doctors' verdict was anything but absolutely correct, but I do know that when I got the summons to go home God gave me a different order, and I remained until some eighteen months afterwards."

Studd did go on furlough for a brief time and when he returned to Africa it was with eight new helpers. He again continues: "Up till that time, though my wife worked for the whole day and worked hard, she was unable to arise till the mid-day prayer meeting much less able to speak at one.

"Surely God was waiting for some act of faith to send down His cyclone of blessing. That cyclone hit my wife the very day after I left, and she was never the same woman again. There was no invalid about her; she became a cyclone, became the Mission's chief deputation secretary as well as a great many other things besides. She was the chief speaker at all our annual and other public meetings.

"She had often wanted to come out here but that I would never allow, for I knew it was mere suicide on her part: she could never have stood the heat. Moreover, I knew she would be of far more service to

God and the Mission and even to me at home and elsewhere than out here….She went to Canada, Australia, New Zealand, Tasmania and South Africa. She lived with no other thought than the salvation of souls and the looking after her children.

"Some will ask, 'How did you in the end permit her to come to the heart of Africa?' It is well that question should be answered. When we were first married we entered into a contract with God that we would neither of us ever keep the other back from doing any work that God laid before us. God was wonderfully gracious. All our earlier years He had kept us together: in China ten years; in India seven years, and in between times in England. Then came the founding of this Mission; but when that took place neither of us dreamed that it would involve a very long separation.

"The state of my health seemed to forbid such a thing absolutely, but 'God works in mysterious ways His wonders to perform.' I did not expect to stay one year the first time out; I remained two. My second innings is still proceeding. It is now over thirteen years since I left England for the last time. The years have been added one by one, and then it came about some two years ago that my wife was traveling with a great friend of hers through the Mediterranean and landed in Egypt.

"The question of our meeting whether in Egypt or here, naturally came into our minds. I could not leave to go to Egypt. The opening of motor roads had made it possible for my wife to be here in two days. I wired and wrote an invitation for her to come, not only from myself but from all the missionaries on the Field. I knew perfectly well that she wanted me to come home, but I knew that would never do and I knew that her permanently staying in the heart of Africa was an impossibility. If she did not return to England she would have very speedily gone to Heaven. And so I said, 'Come, we will all pray together, we will baptize our lives once afresh as of old. In all our young days God kept us together, now it is a small thing that He should ask, in our old age, that we should yield each other up to Him to execute this work of evangelization. We will meet together once again, and then we will part for ever till we meet in Heaven—you to do the work in England that I am convinced nobody else can do but you, and I to do the work here that is equally demanded of me.'

"She came. It was a joy to be on the same platform with her again, but her presence was an agony to me all the time, for plainly I could see the terrible cost to her of every day, yea hour, that she spent here.

"She pleaded with me to be allowed to stay; she almost became rebellious, and then how she prayed that I would go home with her, and assured me that the work would go on just the same here. But there is never any doubt in one's mind when the real word of command from God comes. That command came to me and it was 'Stay!'

"And so it was that we parted. I can only be thankful to God that He was gracious enough to take her to Himself without letting her go through what would have been so terrible to her, a long illness compelling her to inactivity."

C. T. Studd had meant business when he consecrated his life to the Savior of men. His wealth, his ease, his friends, his career—all were placed at the disposal of the Lord. Having sacrificed a fortune and position, it was not odd that he should fail to understand how so many other missionaries endeavored to establish on a foreign field, in the midst of such great poverty and want, the luxuries and standards of the Western World. For them he showed openly his disdain by choosing for himself and his family the pilgrim life.

How well I remember being deeply touched by this man's self-denial when reading his biography. It was not his success as the founder of a mission that touched my heart, but the Spartan-like living quarters of the man who was leader. A small room, a mud floor, a simple rope bed, a chair and a desk—these comprised all that the founder of what is now "Worldwide Evangelization Crusade," needed.

Well then, did Studd find the battle ease up a bit as he neared the end? Never! Not long before his death, Studd almost broke his heart over the threatened action taken by members of his home committee to take over the Heart of Africa Mission. A godly man of some influence stepped in and gave timely advice as well as support to Studd's son-in-law which saved the hardly won venture from disaster.

Nevertheless, Studd felt the impact to the end, stunned and incredulous that his friends should act thus. The betrayal of his one-time supporters broke his heart which never did heal. Only death brought relief to the warrior. Words of his own reveal the extent of this bruising: "Sometimes I feel and especially of late, that my cross is heavy beyond endurance, and I fear I often feel like fainting under it, but I hope to go on and not faint. My heart seems worn out and bruised beyond repair, and in my deep loneliness I often wish to be gone, but God knows best, and I want to do every ounce of work He wants me to do."—C. T. Studd, pp. 212

> Don't seek a long life—Christ had a short one.
> Don't live in luxury—Christ lived and died poor.
> Don't live in pleasure—Christ pleased not Himself.
> Don't live for fame—Christ made Himself of no reputation.
> Don't live at ease—Christ suffered for you the shame
>   and the scourge of the Cross.
> Don't lose your opportunity and inherit an eternity of shame
>   and regrets hereafter.
>
> —C. T. Studd

VIVIAN DAKE
CALLS BACK

"Wherefore Jesus also, that he might sanctify the people with his own blood, suffered without the gate. Let us go forth therefore unto him without the camp, bearing his reproach."

HEBREWS 13:12-13

VIVIAN DAKE was up to an awkward decision. Which pathway would he take? The one road led to honors within his own denomination; the other was outside the camp of his former friends and religious associates. Writing in a letter to someone at this time he explains his dilemma: "I saw the honors of the church. I was wanted in three different conferences to take chairmanship. I was also wanted to take charge of two seminaries. To go into Band Work was the way of the cross, the way of reproach and shame. I knew many of my friends would turn yet God seemed to be holding me to it."

A cheering voice came from his former minister friend who urged him to, "Organize your bands. Push out. Be as aggressive as the Salvation Army, but more holy, more serious and have no nonsense about it."

Vivian Dake was only in his early thirties when this choice confronted him. He had already experimented in the Band Work, organizing young people into groups of four and sending them into districts where the Gospel needed to be preached in power. Vivian Dake hated formalism and he also had little use for the shallow altar methods employed all about him.

But there were those who accused the young man of wishing to split the denomination through using such unorthodox methods. They could not attribute the hot love he had to God and souls to anything other than an unholy ambition to start a new church. Many strenuously opposed him, and even some of those who had been his good friends left him to tread the lonely road outside the religious camp. In this way he came to know the fellowship of His Savior Who likewise had gone outside the camp during His brief life.

That lonely road that had all the marks of the cross, eventually led the self-denying, self-sacrificing young soul-winner to the shores of Africa. He was not there long before fever racked his body and friends put him on the steamer thinking that the good sea air would revive him, but the courageous warrior died on board ship, as far as we know, alone. Word, however, did reach friends at Sierra Leone that Vivian Dake had passed on to be with the Lord, and they met the boat when it docked and gave his body a Christian burial.

This young missionary was only thirty-eight years old, but he had matured far beyond his years and grasped the meaning of the cross deeply. Here are some pointed words he wrote about the position "outside the camp."

"Only be sure that you follow the Master, that your lives tell for Him, and you will find Him also outside the camp. Let not the one who loves popularity think to find it in the way of the Nazarene. He will find the joy that the world knows not of; he will find the way of Life, but the applause of the world goes in another line. This is the line where comes the glory. The saints of God find it better to take it and the glory that follows, than to have an empty profession without God in the soul.

"We cannot be saved by companies. We must learn to stand alone. It is pleasant to have good companionship, but the child of God is ready to stand alone in the breach. Some are good soldiers in a crowd; but how few can follow Jesus alone when all the reproach falls on their devoted heads. It means to receive the multitudes' reproach. Some think that because the multitudes reproach you, you must be wrong. Jesus received the reproach of the throng; so must those who go with

Him. It will come seemingly like an overflowing tide, and the weak and faint-hearted will fall in with it. But the resolute few will boldly withstand it for Jesus' sake."

> Outside the camp unto Thy dear Name,
>   This in Thy Word I see,
> Unto that Name, then I share in His shame,
>   Privileged place to be.
> Feasting on Christ, His reproach to share,
>   Tempt not my soul away,
> Naught can compare with the blessedness there,
>   Outside the camp with Thee.
>
> Outside the camp unto Thy dear Name,
>   Lord, may I here be found.
> Weaned from the world, all its pomp and its fame,
>   Resting on holy ground.
> Outside the camp, in Thy company till
>   Earth's little day be done,
> Then face to face, all Thy mercies to trace,
>   Inside the camp with Thee.
>
> —Fred Magee

"To go forth unto Him without the camp," said Oswald Chambers, "bearing His reproach, does not mean going outside the worldly crowd; it means being put outside the religious crowd you belong to. One of the most poignant bits of suffering for a disciple comes along that line. If you remain true to Jesus Christ there are times when you will have to go through your convictions and out the outer side, and most of us shrink from such a step because it means going alone. The 'camp' means the religious set you belong to; the set you do not belong to does not matter to you."

Another well-known Englishman, F. B. Meyer, author and convention speaker, has written in one of his books about the lonely road outside the camp that always leads to the cross:

"The policy of going forth without the camp is the only safe course for ourselves, as it is the only helpful one for the world itself. There are plenty who argue that the wisest policy is to stop within the camp, seeking to elevate its morals. They do not realize that, if we adopt their advice, we must remain there alone for our Lord has already gone. It is surely not befitting that we should find a home where He is expelled. What is there in us which makes us so welcome, when our Master was cast out to the fate of the lowest criminals?"

OSWALD CHAMBERS CALLS BACK

"The darkness and the light are both alike to thee."

PSALMS 139:12

"Thou hast hid their heart from understanding."

JOB 17:4

REMEMBER so well Mr. Chambers giving us a bit of his personal experience, and saying that after being much used in preaching and seeing many converted through his ministry, there settled down on him a great darkness—that lasted not for days only but for years. He told me that the words 'darkness and light are both alike to thee,' had been such a help to him; and that eventually he came out of the shadows with a more steadfast faith and a balance that was not disturbed by things that formerly would have affected him temperamentally. I think it was this characteristic of his life that proved such a blessing to many as they came in contact with him.—Ashley King

> All else may go if I may have but Thee;
> My heart, tho' desolate, be unafraid,
> Thro' depths of loneliness still undismayed
> If Thou be with me, guiding, holding me;
> The loss but now sustain'd is no more loss;
> No burden any longer is this Cross.
>
> The joys that were denied have left me free
> To fix my heart, my hopes, my love on Thee;
> My sainted dead stand midway to the height
> Of joys eternal, changeless, infinite;
> But none too close may stand, nor come between,
> Lest Thy blest Face should be less clearly seen.

All else may go if I may have but Thee,
For Thou art the beginning and the end
Of my desire, dearer than any friend,
Closer than all in spirit-unity;
Deeper than tenderest human trust shall lie
Within my soul Thy changeless Verity.

—G. M.

Victor Hugo was one of France's most popular literary figures, then came exile from his native land and friends. Napoleon had suspicioned Hugo's political leanings and so punished him, as he thought, by banishment. But Hugo discovered his true self during this time and wrote *Les Miserables*, his most famous novel. Twenty years after being exiled he exclaimed, "Why was I not exiled before?"

FLORENCE ALLSHORN CALLS BACK

"And hast borne, and hast patience, and for my name's sake hast labored, and hast not fainted."

REVELATION 2:3

"THE DIFFICULTIES of driving a car have been exaggerated," said the learner to his driving instructor after he had started, backed, stopped and turned with ease in the country.

His teacher did not comment but suggested they leave the country and try driving in crowded, city traffic. Cars were in front, behind and whizzing by with such speed that the perspiring new driver stopped on a side road exclaiming, "If it were not for other people!"

"Yes," smiled his teacher, "that's about all there is to driving a car: other people."

Many a young missionary has found their work fairly uncomplicated but for "other people."

"The 'plague of flies' was not peculiar to Egypt—you will find them in the shape of busy little people that try to get over the windows of your soul and irritate your outlook," said Oswald Chambers. Such an experience is common to missionaries and pastors. The following is written by Dr. Lambert on the experience of Florence Allshorn, and how she overcame a most trying position on the mission field that had overwhelmed seven others before her. How she overcame is most encouraging:

"Florence Allshorn was the daughter of a doctor whose practice was in the East End of London. She lost both her father and her mother before she was four years old. Along with her two brothers, she was brought up by a kindly, but unimaginative, friend of the family who did not realize how much Florence lacked a mother's love.

"Dr. Gresford Jones and his wife were friends who greatly influenced her life. She threw herself into active service for Christ, working among the rough factory girls and leading the Sunday School. In 1920, the missionary call became clear and she offered herself as a missionary candidate to the Church Missionary Society. She was appointed to Uganda and sent out without further training. There she found a well-established mission field, with a wonderful tradition. Nevertheless, there was much that was professional and superficial which grated on the keen, eager spirit of the new missionary. Here is a typical extract from one of her early letters:

"'I need God so much here. Everything is so difficult. There is so much "ungoodness" in everything. I keep reminding myself that I am here for Christ and that all the wild and miserable things, as well as the holy and calm ones, must beat through me if I am to be used at all. And I thank God that I am here and that it isn't easy. I always wanted that.'

"'The greatest problem was not "loneliness, disheartening work, language, rats in your bedroom, wild beasts in the garden, ants, bites by the hundreds." In spite of these she says: "I have really been happier this month than I ever have been before. The real problem was that of a strained relationship with a senior colleague. Long afterwards, Miss Allshorn told the story of what happened, and of how it became a crisis in her experience:

"'I was young and I was the eighth youngster who had been sent, none of whom had lasted more than two years. I went down to seven stone (98 pounds) and my spirit and soul wilted to the same degree.

"'Then one day the old African matron came to me when I was sitting on the verandah crying my eyes out. She sat at my feet and after a time she said, "I have been on this station for fifteen years and I have seen you come out, all of you saying you have brought to us a Savior, but I have never seen this situation saved yet."

"'It brought me to my senses with a bang. I was the problem for myself. I knew enough of Jesus Christ to know that the enemy was the one to be loved before you could call yourself a follower of Jesus Christ, and I prayed, in great ignorance as to what it was, that this same love might be in me, and I prayed as I have never prayed in my life for that one thing. Slowly things righted. Whereas before she had been going about upsetting everybody with long, deep, dreadful moods, and I had been going into my school depressed and lifeless, both of us found our way to lighten each other.'

"For a whole year, Florence read 1 Corinthians 13 every day. She was learning the meaning of true love, the love of God shed abroad in the heart. Meanwhile, she was doing a grand work in charge of the Girls' Boarding School and, at the same time, training teachers. She was learning also to love the African.

"After four years, Florence Allshorn was back on furlough. Through her experiences on the mission field, she had come to a deep knowledge of Christ, but her body was weak and the future was uncertain. A specialist, diagnosing tuberculosis, wanted her to have a serious operation. She, however, was led to put her trust in God for healing and after a time in a Sanatorium she was wonderfully restored. The Church Missionary Society asked her to act as a Temporary Warden in charge of their Women Candidates. Thus unknowingly she entered upon her life's work.

"Meanwhile, out of the upset and limitations of those days, there came a new vision. Florence Allshorn realized the need of missionaries on furlough, many of them frustrated and aware of their spiritual barrenness. The outcome of this vision was the opening of a Community House known as St. Julian's where those in spiritual need of rest and renewal could come and live in fellowship.

"Her great contribution to the work of missionary training was the emphasis on the working out of the Christian message in human relationships. The one remedy was a drastic dealing with self—'the "I" ingrained in every beat of our hearts, every movement of our minds, every habit of our habitual days.'"

—*The Flame,* Dr. Lambert with remarks
taken from Florence Allshorn by J. H. Oldham

GRANT COLFAX TULLER CALLS BACK

"God my maker...giveth songs in the night."

JOB 35:10

"The Lord will command his lovingkindness in the daytime, and in the night his song shall be with me."

PSALMS 42:8

WHEN SINGING hymns that deeply move us, we can be assured that the music and words poured forth from a suffering-hearted composer. When Grant Colfax, the writer of 5,000 hymns and the composer of the music for that grand old hymn, "Face to Face," was interviewed, he revealed the unusual form of suffering which he had experienced from childhood.

When only two years of age, Grant's mother died and he was left in the care of his father who, through wounds received in the Civil War, was unable to gain his living by hard work and who found his young son to be a rather heavy load and often left him with kind neighbors for short periods of time. These gradually lengthened into much longer periods until Grant eventually lost track of his father's whereabouts.

He relates one incident which indelibly left its impress on both mind and body: "Several places they were kind to me, and other places they were not, and always, I had to work hard. One man was kind enough when he was not drunk, but he was seldom sober. His favorite way of punishing me, if I did some trifling thing to displease him, was to hang me up by my thumbs, a rope around each thumb, pulled up until my toes just barely touched the floor. There I would hang for several hours and one day they went off leaving me hanging for nine hours!

"When I was finally taken down, my thumbs were black, and when I lay down in bed, I could not let my arms lie down—had to keep them up as they had been all day! The effects of that day's hanging have lasted through life, by way of a poor heart."

After Grant Colfax Tuller's conversion as a young man, he commenced preaching. On one occasion, he was to be confronted with the very man who had administered such harsh treatment to him when an orphan. Again Grant Tuller takes up the story:

"I had not seen the last of my old friend who had delighted to hang me up by my thumbs. When preaching in a certain place, and before I had very many texts to preach from, I was standing back of the pulpit, leaning over my Bible before the service began. Looking down into the audience I saw a familiar face. Instantly I was thrown into a state of great excitement.

"Ever since I had received that cruel treatment, I had vowed that if I ever saw that man I would beat him up to within an inch of his life; I had nursed hatred for him in my heart. And here he was before me! I was in an awful turmoil of mind!

"I prayed asking God to give me a text I could preach from for him. Leafing through my Bible, I found this text underlined with red ink 'Thou art weighed in the balances and art found wanting.' I prayed hard and preached.

"When I was through, I gave the call to come to the altar for any who might feel they needed God and we would pray together. The first one to come was that man and his wife! I went down off the platform between them. There I poured out my heart, asking God to forgive me for harboring hate all those years and asking God to save this man. He did both. I did not beat that man; God attended to that for me! That poor sinful man had a miracle of grace performed in his heart—he was a new man!"

'Twas in the darkness I learned it,
　　The song of anguish and pain,
With notes of exquisite sweetness,
　　Distilled in the storm and the rain,
The school of sorrow was needed
　　To tune my voice for the song;
My Heav'nly Father's the Teacher,
　　The lessons were hard and long.

He molded my voice in the valley,
　　Enriched the chords in the cloud;
The frost brought out the expression—
　　And mellowed the tones so loud.
There are depths in the scale of sorrow
　　Nor angel nor seraph can reach—
Those only who've trodden this earth-scene,
　　Know what the darkness can teach.

For invisible choirs I'm training,
　　The Song of the Lamb they sing;
No jarring sound in that symph'ny,
　　Each note doth with ecstasy ring.
Christ sounded the chord that was lowest,
　　When on the rude Cross He hung;
Hence by the redeemed on earth only
　　Can the song in the night be sung.

　　　　　　　　　　　—Essie Bernstein

EDITH HICKMAN DIVALL CALLS BACK

"I Paul, the prisoner of Jesus Christ."

EPHESIANS. 3:1

For quite a number of years the poetry of Edith Hickman Divall strongly appealed to me, but I had never heard of her or known when she had lived or where. And then, while holding a series of services in a coastal town in the south of England, I met her adopted daughter who introduced me to a collection of her poems. Later, in a letter to me, she divulged the imprisoning circumstances which had plunged that young poetess into depths of pain and suffering. Out of that pressure, the young teenager came to an amazing understanding of God.

When Edith's two maiden aunts, living on a small farm, were needing some assistance to help run that small-holding, her parents sent her, their eldest daughter, to live with and assist these two relatives. But the aunts had no experience with raising growing children so Edith experienced cold, hunger and other hardships over the eleven months she spent with them as she cared for the farm animals and did the daily household chores. Added to his, Edith was a delicate girl, suffering from violent headaches every eighth day which usually lasted three days. This meant that she was rarely free from pain and discomfort.

While walking over the fields in the Romany Marches and suffering from loneliness, hardship and physical weakness, her pent-up spirit would find relief in composing poems which would eventually be printed in the tens of thousands and enrich and comfort many who read them.

"You truly recognized," wrote her adopted daughter, "that unless Auntie had suffered and been chastened herself, she could not have written to help others as she had done over the years. There were ten volumes of her poems printed by the National Sunday School Union."

This poem tells how relief came to Edith when she realized that it was the Lord Who was her prison-keeper:

> If I am in Thy prison, shall I haste
>   To break the bonds wherein Thou holdest me?
> Shall I not rather wait in patience here
>   Until the time when Thou wilt set me free?
>
> It changes all, when I remember this—
>   That Thou art keeping me; I am not here
> In chains which other hands have forged for me:
>   I am Thy captive, and I feel no fear.
>
> Thy love has broken this proud spirit, Lord;
>   And in no sad reluctance now I wait
> But joyfully, and count all honor mine,
>   Because Thy hand has closed my prison gate.
>
> I will be patient! Life is best for me
>   As Thou, in Thy great wisdom, Lord, hast planned.
> It is enough that Thou hast called me here—
>   Albeit yet I may not understand.

In another of her poems she shows the reader how she had attained to the hidden meaning of the Cross:

> The glorious triumph and the song—
> The gifts of God to me belong,
> The place of honor is my right—
> Partaker with the saints in light.
>
> Who would not die for such a life?
> Who would not dare the present strife
> For such a victory as this—
> For such an end of crowning bliss?

They told me only of the cross,
Of shame and sorrow, pain and loss.
They told me—and mine eyes were dim—
That I must give up all for Him.

O crowning glory of the cross!
O wondrous gain from all my loss!
I come, and lo, all things are mine!
Yea!—all things in the life Divine.

All things are mine—not far away,
Hereafter—here and now—today!
On earth I reign in life by One;
Complete, accepted, in God's Son.

—Pickering and Inglis
USED BY PERMISSION

Count it all joy. This, I say, is stern doctrine. To count it all joy when suffering comes upon us, and suffering that tests our faith, how is this possible? It is only possible when we come to think of our righteousness as being infinitely more precious than comfort, happiness or peace; when we come to see that the great thing for us in this life is not to enjoy ease and prosperity, to get rich, to rise in this world, but to become better men. For this we require wisdom—a true estimate of the nature and ends of human life.—R. W. Dale

BE THANKFUL for the FRIENDS who have FORGIVEN you.
for the ENEMIES who keep you CAUTIOUS.
for the DIFFICULTIES that make you STRUGGLE.
for the EMERGENCIES that make you THINK.
for the HARDSHIPS that make you STRONG.
for the DISAPPOINTMENTS that make you TRY HARDER.

CLARA LANGFORD CALLS BACK

"And she was a widow.....And when the Lord saw her, he had compassion on her, and said unto her, Weep not."

LUKE 7:12-13

CLARA LANGFORD was a Somerset school mistress when Henry Simpson, a young Cliff College (Methodist) evangelist came to her village of Timsbury, near Bath, to hold services. She assisted as organist in his services and in due time these two were happily married. For many years, Clara Simpson wrote poetry for *Joyful News*, the organ of Cliff College. She rose most mornings before six o'clock, and it was in these early hours of precious communion with her God that inspiration came for many of her choicest poems. After some years, her beloved husband met with an accident which caused much suffering and eventually resulted in his death. Here she tells how God helped her meet the dark hours of loneliness which followed:

> "Oh, has He planned it right when darkness falls,
> And all one's world which once looked fair and bright
> Had faded out of sight and sorrow reigns?
> He's planned it right."

"Thus I wrote in my darkest hours," Clara continues, when deepest sorrow and loss had touched my life, changing everything. Those of us who have suffered in this way, know how the sorrow returns like a flood to be fought by faith and prayer. It was so with me one May Sunday morning in the early days of my grief. I woke with a sense of depression. Rising early I dressed, made a cup of tea on my stove in my tiny bungalow—I could not eat—and gathering up my

Testament, notebook and pencil, put on coat and hat, locked my door and set out to walk, in the loneliness of my spirit.

"It was a perfect morning and the countryside was lovely. I skirted the village for the woodland road. As I stood on the brow of the first meadow, with a sob in my throat, I said aloud, 'Father Thou knowest, I am so distressed, so lonely, almost heart-broken, and the way seems very difficult—speak to me this morning before I return.'

"Then I wended my way down into the valley. A gate led into a peaceful and picturesque old lane shaded by trees. A stream sang its way through the meadow close by. Oh, the peace and loveliness of that morning as I slowly walked along that lane—walked with a sad, lonely heart and all the time, though I knew it not, my prayer was being answered.

"A little further on the lane widened into a woodland road and a gap in the hedge revealed a small clearing among the trees and a fallen ivy-covered tree trunk lay invitingly a few yards away, so I went in and sat on it.

"Looking around I saw young fern fronds springing up in clusters and at a short distance a large furze bush in all bright yellow blossom. I listened to the birds' songs. I longed with an unspeakable longing for the touch of a vanished hand and the sound of a voice that was still, until I broke into uncontrollable sobbing until I was spent.

"Presently, I opened my Testament, asking for a message. My eyes lighted on St. Paul's words to the Philippians, 1:12, 'But I would ye should understand, brethren, that the things which have happened unto me have fallen out rather unto the furtherance of the Gospel.' Oh, here was strength indeed!—Might not I too, make a pearl out of my grain of sand? I prayed that it might be so and that He would strengthen my heart—give me a new message.

"I lifted my eyes to the tops of the tall trees, beautiful in their new spring dress, then at the glorious blue of the sky above—I thought

of life's journey, now so lonely without the dear one who had made
life rich and beautiful and in the intensity of my spirit I said, 'Oh,
Father, do you know when hearts are aching?' Immediately another
line came—I found notebook and pencil and discovered I was writing
a poem.

"How long I sat there I cannot say, but verse by verse the
inspiration came until it was finished and when I read the lines through
I knew with a deep sense of gratitude and thanksgiving that God had
indeed spoken to me that morning.

"And so it proved. It was requested—together with another
poem—'Answered prayer'—and was produced—beautifully
illustrated in *Golden Thought Series* under the title of *Solace, A Little
Book of Comfort*. Much blessing attended the publication of this little
book. Over the world it went until more than one hundred and fifteen
thousand copies had sold and countless messages were received, but I
shall never know here, all that resulted through His leading that May
Sunday morning.

"It is the first time I have told this story thus. I do so now hoping
hearts that are lonely, troubled, bereaved, disheartened perhaps, may
be helped and find solace and comfort through renewed faith and trust.
'God is able to use you according to His power and not according to
your weakness.'"

Here is the poem:

> Oh Father, do You know when hearts are aching;
>> When summer days have fled and north winds blow,
> Skies heavy, gray, and days so dark and lonely?
>> "My Child, I know."
>
> Oh Father, do You care when hours are empty,
>> Empty of all that made this world so fair—
> When blessings once so precious, now have faded?
>> "My Child, I care."

Oh Father, must we trust when ties are broken,
　　When loves of earth once strong and deep have gone,
And strange unwelcome things beset our pathway?
　　　"Yes, Child, trust on."

"Be of good cheer, Let not your heart be troubled.
　　Nothing can touch your life unless I will;
I, who have shared Life's loneliness and sorrow,
　　　Say 'Peace be still.'"

Father, I will believe; oh, keep me faithful
　　Through life's long day till setting of the sun;
And may I hear when dawns the eternal morning,
　　　"My Child, Well Done."

　　　　　　　　　　—*Joyful News*, Cliff College
　　　　　　　　　　USED BY PERMISSION

DOCTOR CULLIS OF BOSTON CALLS BACK

"Would God I had died for thee."
2 SAMUEL 18:33

"I shall not die, but live, and declare the works of the Lord."
PSALMS 118:17

DR. CULLIS had all that a young physician could wish: a lovely wife, a comfortable home, good and kind friends and a growing practice. Then the blow fell, for his marital happiness was of but a brief duration. The grief-stricken young doctor rehearses the nightmare of sorrow which followed:

"Our marriage and the subsequent death of my dear wife had a wonderful influence upon me in preparation for the then unknown future. I loved my wife with all my heart; she was dearer to me than life itself; a perfect idol and I would gladly have died with her. I had gone on into practice, and on my wife's account still remained in the office of her brother-in-law until after her death.

"My first uplifting out of sorrow, suffering and dread was transitory, a dream which soon passed away. When my wife was laid low, it was the funeral of the new life I had begun to live in her. The separation between her soul and body was not more real than that which it caused between my soul and the world. I died in that hour to the main object of my life, and was buried with my wife to the new life I had just begun to live.

"But alas I did not die to sin, nor did I rise to God in Christ Jesus. Shall I explain? It was like this. During the bright months of our wedded life, the future for the first time loomed up before me like a panorama, each changing step in our progress unfolding a picture of beauty. An independent practice; a delightful office and home rented; a name; a lucrative career; a home of our own with every luxury and convenience; and finally retirement amid the laurels of success and the pleasures of abundance.

"In each of these pictures, the central group were two figures entwined in one, and when one of those figures came to be blotted out it blotted out the whole; every picture became simply hideous. The future became to me a dread and like a burden. I would have hailed death as the king of delights but it would not come. I was alive and could not die.

"I felt confident that money would flow in upon me. What should I do with it? During the dark hours while the lifeless form of my wife was still above ground, I was much in the room where we had laid it, and there those reflections ripened into purpose and the purpose took the form of a vow saying, 'Lord, my wife is dead and I have no one now to make money for. I will give all I receive over my expenses for Thy cause.' It was a sort of a slave's vow to a distant master, with little in it with reference to the personal relations which ought to have been accepted between God and myself. A cold vow of money to the cause of a distant Lord; that was all. It was the seal of my own vow to the death of my soul to the world. And as such it was a great step toward the unseen goal before me of complete self-abandonment to Christ in preparation for His work.

"Soon my hands were full, and a surplus of money began to flow in. My vow was kept. I scattered tracts by thousands. I bestowed money right and left to every Christian cause, without letting my right hand know what my left hand gave.

"Yet I was not happy; indeed I was miserable and every day of my life I wished myself dead. It was a slave's life that I led. Selfishness was not dead; pride was not dead; vanity was not dead; envy and malice and the whole brood of vipers which are born of self, still lived. As for the love of Christ, I did not comprehend it, nor had responsive love been yet awakened in my heart for Christ in any considerable degree.

"Dissatisfaction with my state of mind gradually and insensibly came upon me like hunger while one sleeps and desire for deliverance sprang up and grew, I scarcely knew how. My eyes began to be opened to the fact that of all I gave to the cause of Christ a large percentage was used to keep open the receiving and disbursing channels. I longed for some changed policy. I was, in fact, thoroughly dissatisfied with the way my earnings were used and perfectly disgusted with myself. Two desires, one for purity of heart, and the other for an unwasting channel for my gifts, sprang up and grew together simultaneously. I began to really pray. Then the Lord began to open my eyes to the Scriptures to something more than a great field to be gone over piecemeal day by day as the slave hoes a field of corn so much daily as his task.

"I took the Bible in my two hands, closed it, held it up thus and said, 'I do and will forever, by God's grace, believe every word between these two lids, whether I understand it or not. I will take every precept and promise in the Bible as my own, just as if my own name, Charles Cullis, was written in every one of them.'

"First, God unfolded clearly and fully to me the fact that He Himself is my righteousness; that in Him, not in myself, I am justified; and that in Him, not in myself, I have eternal life. He caused me to see that he who believes in the Son of God hath life—hath life already— whilst he that believeth not in Him hath not life. It was a wonderful advance, a great and glorious step out from under the law into grace for salvation.

"The keeping power of Christ was the second great lesson taught me by the Lord. I knew my need of being kept, but thought at first that it could only be met by a greater vigilance in self-keeping; and a greater firmness of self-reliance and determination; but this failed me.

"Finally one day, while repeating the Lord's Prayer, the petition, 'Keep us from evil,' seemed instinct with a significance I had never before apprehended. The evil it refers to I had always until then supposed to be that which is external to us, and which comes upon us without our choice—accident, diseases, losses, and the like. But then I saw it to refer to evil in the heart, evil in the disposition, evil in the spirit. I saw that, like the petition, 'Let thy kingdom come,' it related primarily to our inner life, not to the outward circumstances.

"Then this new light was sealed home to me by the Spirit, in the words, 'For thine is the kingdom, and the power, and the glory, forever and ever. Amen.' I saw that the kingdom within is the Lord's, and the power to set it up, and to keep it up forever and ever is His also. Not the helping power to self-keeping, but the keeping power altogether. When I saw this I said with all my heart, 'Yea, Lord. The power that keeps is a power that illuminates, subdues, teaches, strengthens, upholds, guides, sweetens, enlivens, gives peace and everything else that pertains to God's kingdom within. I do not see how I ever lived without it and I am sure that but for this I should have been poorly prepared for the dear work the Lord has called me to do."

Dr. Cullis was led into a faith work in establishing a hospital for sufferers of consumption. His clear guidance into this work is but a continuance of his clear perceptions of that grace which enabled him to undertake the work. Dr. Cullis calls back to other mourners: Discover the loving purposes of God in your bereavement and turn your losses into heavenly gains.

> God is enough!
>   Though all else besides be changed—
> These earth lights dimmed,
>   And human friends estranged,
> And all the road before thee
>   Dark and rough—
> What then? The best remains:
>   God is enough!

125

Turn from the wreck of all that lies below;
Lift up thine eyes unto His face, and know
That in Himself alone all good is stored—
All, all for thee—and worship thou the Lord.

—Edith Hickman Divall
USED BY PERMISSION

"His love broke my heart," said a Christian, "to make room for Christ, and I know it was love that did it. Till then, I never knew either the creature's need of Christ, nor Christ's sufficiency for a broken heart."—G. V. W.

HORACE BUSHNELL
CALLS BACK

"Not as though I had already attained, either were already perfect:
but I follow after, if that I may apprehend that for which
also I am apprehended of Christ Jesus."

PHILIPPIANS 3:12

"GOD DOESN'T SEND tragedies into our lives but He sure doesn't like to waste them."—Rev. Bruce Nettleton

Horace Bushnell had an only son, a manly, spiritually-inclined, sweet-natured child on whom the affectionate father had indulged fond hopes. The boy had struggled with various health problems for some time and then, suddenly, developed alarming symptoms of brain disease and died. Inevitably, Horace was devastated and Mrs. Bushnell, who alone knew of her husband's struggles, wrote:

"It was a heavy blow, never to be forgotten, one which influenced his whole future life and character. His thoughts began at once to push on eagerly into the unknown, and he wrote several sermons on the 'Life of Heaven.' When a year or two after, he went into the country to preach for an old friend, the latter noticed an increased fervor in his preaching, and in intimate talk perhaps alluded to it, when he said earnestly, 'I have learned more of experimental religion since my little boy died than in all my life before.'"

Later, Horace Bushnell entered into a deeper experience of the Lord and came to apprehend more clearly God's original destiny for him. Mrs. Bushnell discloses God's gracious dealings with her husband:

"The year 1848 was the central point in the life of Horace Bushnell. It was a year of great experiences, great thoughts, great labors. At its beginning, he had reached one of those headlands where new discoveries open to the sight. He had approached it through mental struggles, trials and practical endeavor, keeping his steadfast way amid all the side-attractions of his ceaseless mental activity.

"Five years before God had spoken personally to him in the death of his beloved little boy, drawing his thoughts and affections to the spiritual and unseen, until, by slow advances, the heavenly vision burst upon him. He might well have said what Edward Irving said of a like sorrow: 'Glorious exchange! He took my son to His own more Fatherly bosom, and revealed in my bosom the sure expectation and faith of His own eternal Son.'

"'I believed,' he afterwards said, 'from reading especially the New Testament, and from other testimony, that there is a higher, fuller life that can be lived and set myself to attain it. I swung for a time towards quietism, but soon passed out into a broader, more positive state.' This phase of feeling, so foreign to his self-reliant, positive nature, served its uses on that very account; but it could not long detain him from the more vigorous faith by which he apprehended Christ as the 'power of an endless life.'

"On an early morning of February, his wife awoke, to hear that the light they had waited for, more than they that watch for the morning, had risen indeed. She asked, 'What have you seen?' He replied, 'The Gospel.' It came to him at last, after all his thought and study, not as something reasoned out, but as an inspiration—a revelation from the mind of God Himself.

"The full meaning of his answer he embodied at once in a sermon on 'Christ the Form of the Soul' from the text 'Until Christ be formed in you.' The very title of this sermon expresses his spiritually illuminated conception of Christ as the indwelling, formative life of the soul—the new, creating power of righteousness for humanity."

Later he explained this experience thus: "I seemed to pass a boundary. I had never been very legal in my Christian life, but now I passed from those partial 'seeings,' glimpses and doubts, into a clearer knowledge of God and into His inspirations, which I have never wholly lost. The change was into faith—a sense of the freeness of God and the ease of approach to Him."

"'Christian faith,' as he says, 'is the faith of a transaction. It is not the committing of one's thought in assent to any proposition, but the trusting of one's being to a being, there to be rested, kept, guided, molded, governed and possessed forever....It gives you God, fills you with God in immediate, experimental knowledge, puts you in possession of all there is in Him, and allows you to be invested with His character itself.'

"The greatness of this change and its profound reality made him a new man, or rather the same man with a heavenly investiture. In this divine panoply, he was sent into the conflict which immediately followed the publication of *God in Christ*, written the same year; and he was able to meet it with the courage and the poise and the consciousness of Divine support and guidance that at length gave him the victory."

"The story is told of a shepherd wise,
Who when the day was done,
Needed to cross a stream to get home;
He led, but the sheep wouldn't come.
So he gently turned to the flock once more,
Knowing that this was best,
He stooped and lifted the tiniest lamb
Holding it safe on his breast;
While he waded the troublesome stream again,
In the light of the setting sun.
This time there was no hesitation at all,
For they followed him, every one!

"Oh! I wonder if Christ our Shepherd Divine
Doesn't work in the self-same way
By taking our dear little lambs to draw
The sheep who have gone astray.

Sometimes He has tried, yes, so very long,
To get us to follow His call
And when everything fails He takes to Himself
The tiniest lamb of all.
To punish us? No. He loves us so much
That He died for our sins to atone;
But He hopes when the lambs are all safe in the fold
That the sheep will follow Him home!"

—Alice Hansche Mortenson
USED BY PERMISSION

SADHU SUNDAR SINGH
CALLS BACK

"I am come to send fire on the earth; and what will I, if it be already kindled? ...Suppose ye that I am come to give peace on earth? I tell you, Nay; but rather division: For from henceforth there shall be five in one house divided, three against two, and two against three."

LUKE 12:49, 51-52

WHEN SADHU SUNDAR SINGH, a wealthy young Sikh in his mid-teens, was convinced of the truth of the Christ of Calvary, he became a completely altered young man. For nine months, his father, uncle and older brother sought to dissuade him from clinging to his new-found faith and urged him to return to the ancient worship of the Sikhs. At first, they used loving entreaty, but when that failed to influence the boy, they heaped all kinds of humiliations upon him. He was eventually disowned and ordered to leave home forever. The food with which they provided him for his journey had been mingled with poison, for the family did not wish to endure the disgrace of owning him as a relative. He survived, but describes the loneliness which he suffered as an exile from his own family:

"I remember the night when I was driven out of my home—the first night. When I came to know my Savior, my father and my brother and my other relations were told of my conversion. At first they did not take much notice; but afterwards they thought that it was a great dishonor that I should become a Christian, and so I was driven out of my home.

"The first night I had to spend in cold weather, under a tree. I had had no such experience. I was not used to living in such a place without shelter. I began to think: 'Yesterday and before that I used to live in the midst of luxury at my home; but now I am shivering here, and hungry and thirsty and without shelter, with no warm clothing and no food.'

"I had to spend the whole night under the tree, but I remember the wonderful joy and peace in my heart, the presence of my Savior. I held my New Testament in my hand. I remember that night as my first night in Heaven. I remember the wonderful joy that made me compare that time with the time when I was living in a luxurious home. In the midst of luxuries and comfort I could not find peace of heart. The presence of the Savior changed the suffering into peace."

Sadhu Sundar Singh now had ample time to spend whole days and even nights in communion with the Lord, but never did the opposition ease off. A threat was made upon his life years later when he was working in Tibet, and this godly Indian evangelist disappeared never to be heard of again. He was presumed dead and his will probated, but it is not really known whether or not this is true. So fared the boy. So fared the grown man in his forties. The Scripture was indeed fulfilled in his life—the sword had severed family relationships, but brought him into a new relationship in the family of Jesus Christ.

As this godly evangelist traveled in the western world, speaking, he was appalled at the materialism which had permeated the general concept of Christianity. In indulging one's love for comforts and luxuries, the ideal of the life of their Leader had become lost to many of His followers. A deplorable deterioration of Biblical standards was the result, and the following incident as told in the *Oriental Missionary Standard* reflects his deep convictions:

"A Bishop was making a plea for dark India, telling in a vivid way of the great need of the 300,000,000 in that land bound by caste and superstition. At the close of his appeal the great audience rose to sing:

"Faith of our fathers, living still,
In spite of dungeon, fire and sword
Our fathers chained in prisons dark
Were still in heart and conscience free.

How sweet would be their children's fate,
If they like them could die for Thee.

"In the congregation sat the Indian Evangelist, Sadhu Sundar Singh. He sprang to his feet shouting, 'Stop singing that! Stop singing that! It is spiritual perjury! Not one of you would die for Him. Nothing but a white corpse will ever convince our people of India that you mean what you are singing.'

"In the audience was a young missionary, James Blackman. He took up the challenge and rising said, 'Let me go back again to India!' He laid his body at Jesus' feet, a living sacrifice, and returned to India. Not for long was he in that most trying climate until cholera broke out among the natives and hundreds were hurried to isolation hospitals—hundreds who had never been given one opportunity to hear the Calvary story. News came to the mission station daily telling of the many deaths, and Someone said to James Blackman, 'I wish to go to the isolation hospital, but I must have feet to walk with, a mouth to speak through.' James Blackman said to his Master, 'I will give You mine.'

"He went and ministered to the sick and the dying, telling them of a Savior's love and of the city yonder where thousands of redeemed ones, washed in the precious blood would enter. He saw many 'look and live.' And then one day he fell ill with the dreaded disease and was placed by Indian nurses in a ward with his brown brethren. In his delirium he called out, 'Did I reach the last one?'

"Sadhu Sundar Sing hurried to the hospital and was shown into the ward where between two of his brethren lay the 'white corpse' of James Blackman. Said the Sadhu, 'Now I see Calvary,' and with a heart pierced by the sorrows of his own countrymen, he went out to lift high the royal banner of the cross and to lay down his own life a living sacrifice—with James Blackman 'filling up that which is behind in the sufferings of Christ.'"

A SINGLE WOMAN CALLS BACK

"Thy Maker is thine husband."

ISAIAH 54:5

DEAR JANE:

Your letter written on Joan's wedding day arrived yesterday and I've thought of it almost continually since. I know how it feels to be maid of honor at a younger sister's wedding, and I appreciate your honesty in describing your mixed emotions.

All of us have to face the possibility that God's plan for our lives may not include marriage, and of course you wonder if there can ever be complete spiritual victory over your natural desire for a husband, a home and children. I'll try, since you ask me, to share with you some of the ways in which God has directed my thinking along these lines.

The fact that you're now twenty-five and not married does not necessarily mean that marriage is not in God's plan for you. You and even I, in spite of my additional twenty years, may find that God has someone for us whom He has not yet brought into our lives. But I believe that you're wise to recognize the possibility of having to spend your life alone, and to face it; to bring this part of your life to Him in complete surrender. You'll find it's something not achieved overnight or arrived at easily; yet the sooner we begin to bring this innermost core of our lives to God in utter relinquishment, the easier it will be to learn that secret of real victory, not only in this area, but in all others.

We don't know why God chooses to give the joys of marriage to some of His children and to withhold them from others, and at first, there's a tendency to feel left out, almost cheated of something that is ours by right.

This painful "Why?" must be brought to God in surrender over and over again as life goes on. Indeed, there is no answer to it on earth. How non-Christians, especially girls, deal with such problems I can't imagine. I'm profoundly thankful that I don't have to do so.

But for us who have committed our lives to God through Jesus Christ there is an answer, and in it is peace. We know that in God's infinite wisdom and sovereignty, His way is perfect, and that one radiant morning in the light of His eternal revelation all such questions will be answered to our utmost satisfaction. How thankful I am that I know Him!

Now supposing that God is calling you to a single life, how can you face it without becoming bitter, frustrated and resentful?

First, of course, as I've already said, you must bring all of your life to God in unconditional surrender, and especially this part with its details and implications.

I think perhaps it's here that some Christian girls fail. Accepting the possibility that they will remain unmarried, they either consciously or unconsciously assume that as a result only a second-best life is open to them, and accordingly they live on the plains instead of finding the wings that God would provide for soaring to the heights. For the mountain peaks of Christian living aren't reserved for the married alone. They are reachable to all who want to appropriate His grace to scale them. And sometimes I think that He has special heights of joy in Himself for those from whom He has withheld the beauties of marriage.

That true Christian marriage is beautiful, no one can deny. It is the highest expression on earth of the relationship between Christ and His Church. To look at it scornfully and say, in effect, "I didn't want that anyway," is to disparage God's loveliest revelation of Himself apart from Christ. Too many single girls adopt this sour grape attitude, but the path to victory doesn't run through that vineyard. We shouldn't be ashamed of our natural desire for marriage, which is God-given and right. But neither should we feel that, lacking such consummation, our lives will be incomplete, for we are complete in Jesus Christ, and the most beautiful marriage on earth is only a shadow of that union with Him which may be experienced by anyone who will earnestly set herself to seek it.

I sometimes wonder if God has withheld marriage from me so that my whole heart may be centered in love for Him. If so, I have "the better part"; for to know Him is the truest satisfaction in life. Not that married people may not or do not know this; many of God's greatest saints have been married. But I can't help noticing the amazing heights reached by certain unmarried women (Amy Carmichael, Mary Slessor, Frances Ridley Havergal, to name a few) and to wonder, at least, if a special fullness of joy and achievement may not be reserved for the unmarried woman who seeks to give herself, soul and body, to the Lord Jesus Christ. I wonder if it is by accident that countless single women are among the greatest names in missionary history, or if it may be for reasons something like this.

The companionship and fellowship of a God-given marriage are a lovely thing. One is never alone for very long. In absence, the partners experience a sweet sense of each other's presence, an overwhelming desire for the beloved one's return. But this is merely a picture, a shadow of the relationship between Christ and His own, of which we may have the very substance. As we realize more and more of His presence, we come to know that we, too, are never alone. Though absent from Him now, our hearts rest in His sweet companionship, and more and more earnestly long for the hour of His return. Death becomes our entrance to His beloved presence.

And these things are not theory. They are reality…the quintessence of Christian experience, as real as marriage itself. They are real enough to take away the chill of entering an empty apartment when you come home from work, real enough to fill lonely evenings with exquisite content. Are they even more real than a companion in the flesh? I do not know; I only know that the companionship of Jesus is real and satisfying. And you may find that reality too, if you come to Him for it.

Every human being longs for another's complete understanding; comparatively few achieve it, even in the sweetest marriage ties. Yet it is ours for the taking. God has not withheld this priceless gift from us just because we are not married. Let us cultivate it, living in its beauty.

What about children? I can hear you ask, for I know how you love them. Surely, you will say, this is one place where only marriage can satisfy the deep longing of every woman to bring other lives into the world, to love and nurture them, to bring them up to know and serve the Savior.

The unmarried woman in union with Jesus Christ will know, richly and abundantly, the joy of creating new life in fellowship with Him. He desires that we bring forth fruit unto eternal life; and if we yield ourselves to Him, He will fulfill His good pleasure through us, and we shall know the holy joys of spiritual motherhood.

Recently I spent a week's vacation with an old school friend who had just recently become a Christian. I have seldom seen such hunger for the things of God. We spent every available moment discussing spiritual things and in prayer and fellowship. How she drank in the things of Christ! I was utterly drained after each long talk, yet exquisitely happy and content; during that beautiful week I wondered if any human mother nursing her child ever knew more joy and satisfaction than I in nurturing this newly-born soul ....

The unmarried woman who has learned to share the life of the Son of God will be able to give to others in their time of need. Not long ago, a young friend of mine lost her baby and I tried to comfort her. Evidently, what I had to say touched her heart, for she burst out: "How can you understand so well? I don't see how anyone who hasn't been through it can possibly know what it's like to lose your baby, but you really seem to know! How can you do it?" I murmured something conventional. But what I could have told her was that any single woman who has relinquished all claims to married happiness and given them back to God has known the death of not one but all her children, of her husband, her home, of all such hopes and dreams. She has, indeed, "been through it," and can enter another's sorrow and bring the comfort wherewith she herself has been comforted by God.

We must remember too, Jane, that not all marriages bring these joys of companionship, fellowship and understanding. Not all wives find love's reward in service. Many are lonely, misunderstood, and serve all their lives for meager thanks. Not all wives become mothers, and of those who do, not all see their children find eternal life in Christ. Surely this must be the greatest of all sorrows.

But for the woman who finds her all in Jesus Christ, satisfaction in all these things is assured. Fellowship and love transcending even the most beautiful human relationship is ours if we will know it. Spiritual motherhood is certain if we know Christ aright, and none of our children will ever be lost to Him.

But are there no regrets? Is it possible always to live in the realm of the spiritual? Have we not physical bodies with physical needs that make themselves felt?

As the years go by, deep insistent voices make themselves heard within us. This undertone can be very strong and it grows with the years. But if we have been living in fellowship with God, our life in Him has been growing too; and if we have trusted Him in this matter early in life and renewed our commitment whenever a new surge of desire or loneliness has arisen, we find that His answer not only keeps pace with these inner questionings, but actually transcends them. At least that has been my experience. It is infinitely easier for me to be unmarried today than it was twenty or even ten years ago. This is not because the human heart becomes less lonely as the years pass—it becomes more so—but my fellowship with Christ is so much deeper now that the voices of loneliness are heard less clearly, even though humanly speaking they may be louder.

A great deal depends upon entering this committed relationship with Christ long before it becomes evident that you are likely to remain unmarried. That's why I'm writing you in such detail. Seek His grace now in this regard. If you marry, this union with Christ will be your greatest assurance of a happy marriage; if you don't marry, it is your only security against a lonely, bitter, barren old age.

—Reprinted by permission from *HIS*, student magazine
of Inter-Varsity Christian Fellowship. Copyright 1958

SAINTS
CALL BACK

"This is life eternal, that they might know thee the only true God, and Jesus Christ, whom thou hast sent."

JOHN 17:3

"I count all things but loss for the excellency of the knowledge of Christ Jesus my Lord: for whom I have suffered the loss of all things, and do count them but dung, that I may win Christ."

PHILIPPIANS 3:8

CHOICE SAINTS throughout the foregoing pages have shared with us their moments of loneliness, and have also confided in us the benefits derived as a result of their suffering. For the most part, they tell us that not until they were emptied of some of the choice treasures of their hearts did they find Christ to be the Altogether Lovely One. They discovered a more intimate relationship with the Almighty God and proved Him to be "their shield and their exceeding great reward."

To miss the friendship of God for any prized earthly gain is loss beyond comprehension. We were created for the sole purpose of communing with God Himself and to partake of the very life of His Son, Jesus Christ. We were purposefully placed in a world antagonistic to good. The Prince of this world was left with the glittering prizes men so esteem and could offer them to each of us tempting us away from the "unseen" realities of eternal worth. The god of this world is God's rival for our love, for our time, for our energy and as such a rival he tempts us with the "seen" so as to engross our attention.

Many a man and woman has been enticed, even though it were for a brief time, from pursuing that friendship with God. The saints who have called back are part of the Church Triumphant, having passed through their probationary period down here. We only pray that the triumph they gained shall urge us to utilize those circumstances which have come or will come to test us, that we might fill up the empty voids with God's fullness rather than seek to cram that bottomless abyss of the soul with transient, earthly persons or things. We were formed to hold the blessed Person of His Son Who alone can satiate and fill the aching void and still the clamoring voices that insistently call for companionship and fulfillment.

G. D. Watson's classic statements on the friendship of God are fitting words with which to conclude this book, and may they bless you as they have blessed us.

"God is the only friend Who never fails us. How frequently and easily the friendships of earth grow threadbare and wear out. As children, we all had little friends that we thought would last forever, but in a few years the delicate romance passed away, and the friends drifted from us.

"Then came youth with its friendships that we thought were rooted in granite, but they obeyed the same law of change and transitoriness.

"And then came middle age life, with its more thoughtful and serious friendships, which after a while were rent with cruel misunderstandings and unexplained silences, and so languidly declined.

"And then we drift on to the lonely quiet havens of old age, into which we anchor our riper years, to find that change and decay have characterized all earthly things, including what we once supposed were friendships riveted with steel.

"It is not always because friends have been unfaithful, but often the pressures of life have separated us. We were but poor creatures, and each has had his special calling, peculiar burdens, diverse paths of travel, and the constant changes of new scenes, new circumstances, new acquaintances, new thoughts, new feelings. Like passing ships at sea, we lived a while in the sight of each other's sails, and enjoyed the beautiful signaling by flags or rockets from soul to soul, but we each had to make a several port, and so we slipped over the rim of the sea, and lost sight of each other.

"But God is the dear old, faithful Friend, from Whom we never sail away, and Who always is going our way, and making for the same port, and Whose interests are always our own. The very things that have killed off the friendship of other people have only made God more and more a friend to us. Just where other friendships wear out, God's friendship wears in. The things that make others forget us are the very things that make God remember us. Just where our failures and infirmities and sorrows over-tax the patience of earthly friends, God's friendship breaks out afresh like finding a gold mine on a place of poor land whose fertility had been exhausted.

"God's friendship was not conditioned on our beauty, or prosperity, or success, or popularity; but on our personality and our being His own creatures who need Him forever. God's friendship for us was never touchy, nor fastidious, nor rash, nor overbearing, nor critical, nor dependent on what other people thought about us. God has proved Himself over and over to be 'the Friend that sticketh closer than a brother.'"—from *Our Own God*

> For the glory and the passion of this midnight
>   I praise Thy name, I give Thee thanks, O Christ!
> Thou that hast neither failed me nor forsaken
>   Through these hard hours with victory overpriced;
> Now that I too of Thy passion have partaken,
>   For the world's sake—called—elected—sacrificed!
>
> Thou wast alone through Thy redemption vigil,
>   Thy friends had fled;
> The Angel at the Garden from Thee parted,
>   And solitude instead.
> More than the scourge, or cross, O Tender-hearted!
> Under the crown bowed down Thy head.

But amid the torture, and the taunting
    I have had Thee!
Thy hand was holding my hand fast and faster,
    Thy voice was close to me;
And glorious eyes said, "Follow me, thy Master,
Smile as I smile Thy faithfulness to see!"

                    —H. Hamilton King

BOOK 3
FRUSTRATION

VICTORIOUS WARRIORS CALL BACK

"Stand ye in the ways, and see, and ask for the old paths,
where is the good way, and walk therein,
and ye shall find rest for your souls."

JEREMIAH 6:16

"Remove not the ancient landmark, which thy fathers have set."

PROVERBS 22:28

THE EARLY ITINERANTS who ministered to the pioneers of this country needed to be God's "no-road" men. A new missionary recruit wrote to C. T. Studd, asking if there were clearly marked roads in the Congo. Studd replied that he wanted "no-road" men for the almost impossible task of pioneering the Congo with the Gospel. One of these hardy itinerants reminisces:

"There were no turnpikes or plank roads throughout the vast field, as a means for easy and rapid travel; but of mud roads as long as the moral law, and nearly as deep as they were long, there were no end. In place of the more elegant and costly turnpike, we had the rustic and heaven-provoking corduroy, which, however, was an excellent antidote to dyspepsia and habits of 'softness and needless self-indulgence,' and was moreover a great promoter of appetite and sound sleep. Those who traveled over these roads needed the apostolic advice, 'Endure hardness as a good soldier of Jesus Christ.'

"In many places there were no roads at all except cow-paths and deer-trails; very often blazed or notched trees were the only indications of the course for the adventurous 'circuit-rider' who wished to pursue from one appointment to another. Many of these blazed pathways are remembered to this day by your humble chronicler, and how his eagerness became more intense as the evening shades began to fall

CALL BACK SERIES · VOLUME 1

more densely on the forest, and the hoot of the night-owl and the weird notes of the whip-poor-will stimulated him to increase his speed."

We make no apology in this *Call Back* for retracing our steps to hear the heart cry of saints who notched and blazed trails for us in this twentieth century. May they beckon to you, uncertain soul, strengthening the cords that bind you to the old cross of Christ. May they give you certainty where doubt has taken over. May you exult that you too are counted worthy to suffer for Jesus, even though many around you would preach another Gospel.

From an old magazine, *The Divine Life*, we culled the following: "The testimony of God's tried and faithful people is of unspeakable value to the whole Church. When these declarations are supported by a lifetime of patient endurance and heroic service for their Master, it is impossible to measure the good effect of their words."

The writer then quotes from Rev. Samuel T. Spear, who had endured many trying adversities, but gained through them inestimable wealth. "In all this sorrow I have been led to study the Bible as never before, and especially all it says of Christ, and my soul has received such a vision of Christ as I had no idea of before....Christ is to me as clear an object of thought, of faith, of affection, and a Being to be served as a personal friend, as plain to me as you—a friend. I lie down with Him. I rise up with Him. I sleep with Him by my side. I walk with Him. I know Him as I never knew Him before, and as I never should have known Him but for the terrible crucifixion of affliction."

> God of all struggling hearts, hold Thou me steady when the
> strain of life lays harsh upon me.
> When work gets harder and hours longer than
> I had expected—
> When illness weakens my body and throws a dark pall over
> my spirit—
> When friends I had trusted fail me—

When the money I had depended upon disappears
    even in the face of my growing needs—
When I find the plans to which I have given my life broken
    to pieces at my feet—
When the pathway of the good life darkens and loses its lure
    for my soul—
Then, Eternal Spirit, steady Thou me for the hard and
    long fight.
Show my soul the spirit of the just and holy men who have
    trodden this rough road before me—
Thread through my hopes the strands of Thy will,
    and presence, and power—
Help me to build the house of my life upon the rock
    of Thy purpose, that the winds and waves destroy it not.
In Christ's Name, I pray. Amen.

—Prophetic News

JOHN WESLEY CALLS BACK

"Son of man, behold, I take away from thee
the desire of thine eyes with a stroke: yet neither shalt thou mourn
nor weep, neither shall thy tears run down."

EZEKIEL 24:16

WHO WOULD have guessed as they watched the imperturbable and undaunted John Wesley preaching at the village cross, that he had experienced a heart-breaking sorrow which had pierced him through and through? God has a Gethsemane for every soul whom He chooses to use. Only broken hearts can minister effectually to a heart-broken humanity.

Through the Wesleys' efforts in London, a young, attractive, well-educated woman had been thoroughly born again. Grace Murray had been married to a Scottish master-mariner from no mean family. When he returned from his duties to find his worldly young wife had turned Methodist, he was furious and threatened to put her into a mental home, but her meek and winsome spirit delayed the execution of his threats.

Putting back to sea, the young mariner was, through some mishap, killed or drowned, and so his widow left London and returned to her native home in Newcastle-on-Tyne. Here she soon found some work to do for the Lord, and on John Wesley's visits there, he employed her as a class-leader of women. Later, he also employed her as housekeeper of a refuge for many tired, wearied and sick itinerants who would sometimes be joined by their families.

Wesley often had reason to reside here on his frequent itinerating visits, and in his journal he betrays the temptation to settle down. "I was ready to say, 'It is good for me to be here,'" he wrote at one time;

"but I must not build tabernacles; I am to be a wanderer upon earth and desire no rest till my spirit returns to God."

During the nine or ten years of Grace Murray's labors, she attained at last the leadership of the women's classes throughout the North of England where she itinerated on horseback, often alone.

It was little wonder that the lonely leader of Methodism should be won by such a woman so devoted to the same cause to which he had consecrated his all. It was not a result of sudden passion that they became engaged, but the outcome of mature judgment after an acquaintance of ten years. John had chosen her to join a little company to travel with him in his journeys, where she could be introduced to a wider Methodist circle. She was now understood by some to be the intended wife of the Founder of Methodism, and there were some good, trusted friends who approved of his choice.

But not so his brother, Charles, who eyed the whole affair with suspicion, perhaps increased by gossips and jealous reactions of members of their Society. Up to the last six weeks before the tragedy struck, Grace Murray had traveled with the undaunted preacher, and their hearts were united in the resolve that nothing would hinder their intended union.

Then Charles intercepted a letter from John directed to Grace Murray. Misinformed as to the truth, he believed that Grace Murray was engaged to one of Wesley's outstanding preachers, John Bennet, and so his impetuous nature determined to put an end to the whole affair. He felt his brother's marriage, under these circumstances, would ruin the cause of Methodism, and so he determined to marry Grace to John Bennet in the absence of his brother.

On October 1, just two days before the wedding, John felt troubled. He records: "I was in great heaviness; my heart was sinking in me like a stone. Only so long as I was preaching I felt ease. When I had done, the weight returned. I went to church sorrowful and very heavy, though I knew not any particular cause. And God found me there.

"The lessons, both morning and afternoon, containing the account of the three children in the fiery furnace, of Daniel in the lions' den, and of our Lord's walking on the water and calming the storm, seemed all designed for me. When I came home, I took up a Common Prayer-Book and opened upon these words: 'Deliver me not over unto the will of mine adversaries; for there are false witnesses risen up against me, and such as speak wrong. I should utterly have fainted; but that I believe verily to see the goodness of the Lord in the land of the living. O tarry thou the Lord's leisure; be strong, and He shall comfort thy heart; and put thou thy trust in the Lord' (Psa. 27:12-14)."

He dreamed that night about Grace Murray. She was condemned to die, and he was watching the execution of that sentence.

On Monday, the 2nd, he fasted, prayed, and felt a will more resigned. The next day, at Leeds, he met George Whitefield but not his brother who was supposed to have been there, but who was resolved not to come until he had seen Grace Murray married.

George Whitefield witnessed how troubled John was and he wept and prayed over John. "But I could not shed a tear," wrote Wesley. "He told me all that was in his power to comfort me, but it was in vain. He told me it was his judgment that she was my wife, and that he had said so to John Bennet; that he would fain have persuaded them to wait, and not to marry till they had seen me; but that my brother's impetuosity prevailed and bore down all before it.

"I felt no murmuring thought, but deep distress. I accepted the just punishment of my manifold unfaithfulness and unfruitfulness, and therefore could not complain. But I felt the loss both to me and the people, which I did not expect could ever be repaired. I tried to sleep, but tried in vain; for sleep was fled from my eyes. I was in a burning fever, and, more and more thoughts still crowding into my mind, I perceived if this continued long it would affect my senses. But God took that matter into His hand, giving me, on a sudden, sound and quiet sleep.

"About eight, one came in from Newcastle and told us, 'They were married on Tuesday.' My brother came an hour after. I felt no anger, yet I did not desire to see him. But Mr. Whitefield constrained me. After a few words had passed, he accosted me with: 'I renounce all intercourse with you, but what I would have with a heathen man or a publican.' I felt little emotion. It was only adding a drop of water to a drowning man, yet I calmly accepted his renunciation, and acquiesced therein. Poor Mr. Whitefield and John Nelson burst into tears. They prayed, cried and entreated till the storm passed away. We could not speak, but only fell on each other's neck.

"John Bennet then came in. Neither of us could speak, but we kissed each other and wept. Soon after I talked with my brother alone. He seemed utterly amazed. He clearly saw I was not what he thought, and now blamed her only, which confirmed me in believing my presage was true, and I should see her face no more."

Charles had believed that his brother was to marry a woman already engaged to another. "Too late," the biographer says, "Charles Wesley discovered that he had persuaded John Bennet to marry his brother's betrothed fiancée and had led Grace to believe that 'the important person' who had steadfastly loved her for ten years had actually expressed the wish that, for the sake of the work of God, she would marry another. It was indeed, not a 'Comedy,' but a 'Tragedy of Errors.'"

Watson in his *Life of Wesley*, (chapter 10), gives an extract from an unpublished letter of Wesley revealing how deeply his heart had been broken, but how resolutely he bore his disappointment. "The sons of Zeruiah were too strong for me. The whole world fought against me, but above all, my own familiar friend (Charles Wesley). Then was the word fulfilled: 'Son of man, behold, I take away from thee the desire of thine eyes with a stroke: yet neither shalt thou mourn nor weep, neither shall thy tears run down.'

"The fatal, irrevocable stroke was struck on Thursday last. Yesterday I saw my friend (that was) and him to whom she is sacrificed. But 'why should a living man complain, a man for the punishment of his sins?'"—*Steven's History of Methodism*

A few stanzas from a poem John composed at this time further reveals the strength of his Gethsemane:

> Amazed I cried, "Surely for me
> A help prepared of Heaven thou art!
> Thankful I take the gift from Thee,
> O Lord, and naught on earth shall part
> The souls that Thou hast joined above
> In lasting bonds of sacred love."
>
> Abashed she spoke: "O what is this?
> Far above all my boldest hope!
> Can God, beyond my utmost wish,
> Thus lift His worthless handmaid up?
> This only could my soul desire!
> This only had I dared require!"
>
> From that glad hour, with growing love
> Heaven's latest, dearest gift I view'd;
> While, pleased each moment to improve,
> We urged our way with strength renew'd,
> Our one desire, our common aim,
> T' extol our gracious Master's Name.
>
> Companions now in weal and woe,
> No power on earth could us divide;
> Nor summer's heat nor winter's snow
> Could tear my partner from my side.

No toils, nor weariness, nor pain
Nor horrors of the angry main.

Oft (though as yet the nuptial tie
   Was not,) clasping her hand in mine,
"What force," she said, "beneath the sky,
   Can now our well-knit souls disjoin?
With thee I'd go to India's coast,
To worlds in distant oceans lost!"

Such was the friend, than life more dear,
   Whom in one luckless, baleful hour,
(For ever mention'd with a tear!)
   The tempter's unresisted power
(Oh the unutterable smart!)
Tore from my inly-bleeding heart!

Unsearchable Thy judgments are,
   O Lord! A bottomless abyss!
Yet sure Thy love, Thy guardian care,
   O'er all Thy works extended is!
O why didst Thou the blessing send?
Or why thus snatch away my friend?

Teach me from every pleasing snare
   To keep the issues of my heart;
Be Thou my Love, my Joy, my Fear!
   Thou my Eternal Portion art!
Be Thou my never-failing Friend,
And love, O love me to the end!

What Thou hast done I know not now;
   Suffice I shall hereafter know!
Beneath Thy chast'ning hand I bow;
   That still I live to Thee I owe.
O teach Thy deeply-humbled son,
Father, to say, "Thy will be done!"

PASTOR HSI
CALLS BACK

"I was a reproach among all mine enemies, but especially among my neighbors, and a fear to mine acquaintance: they that did see me without fled from me...For I have heard the slander of many...while they took counsel together against me"

PSALMS 31:11, 13

PASTOR HSI had been an intelligent scholar in the school of Confucius, the ancient Chinese philosopher, but he was an opium addict and chained to this habit. Then through the inspired efforts of the missionary, David Hill, who was armed with the powerful weapon of God's Word, the proud Chinese scholar was delivered from his evil habit and entered as a little child into the school of Christ.

He now became inspired by a passion to see other afflicted ones also delivered and so in time opened forty-five Refuges to house those desiring to be emancipated from this drug. Hsi's wife also became a true follower of Christ and joined him in this crusade, but among the women. Their pathways often diverged so that at times they only occasionally met for brief intervals when their programs caused their paths to cross.

But Pastor Hsi was not to be exempted from fiery trials and misunderstandings. Satan hates those who demolish his kingdom. There is no true service for Christ and souls that does not stir the anger and bring down the wrath of hell upon such disturbers of Satan's kingdom. It is little wonder therefore that, after some years of this holy warfare, a powerful opposition was roused. Several of Hsi's formerly loyal helpers "turned Judas" and were foremost in the attacks upon him and his work which lasted for two years. To one bent upon only doing good to his fellow-sufferers, it must have broken the heart of Hsi to know that his former associates, who were now his most formidable opponents, should carry their hatred to such extremes as the following incident will illustrate.

Mr. Bagnall, a faithful missionary of the China Inland Mission, received a great shock when there rode up to his Mission Station at Ping Yang a most excited and angry group of Chinamen, some of whom carried knives and other weapons. In their midst sat their prisoner, Pastor Hsi. The puzzled missionary could not make himself heard for some time. The leader of this mob was a man named Fan who himself also had endeavored to do Refuge work. There was a barrage of threats, curses and shouts. Mr. Bagnall later declared that it was a "veritable hell" but he also observed that through it all the prisoner showed the calm which only grace could supply. During the tumult, the missionary had a horse made ready for the prisoner and when the crowd had quieted down a bit, he himself grabbed and held Chang, Fan's accomplice, in spite of his open sword, while signaling to Hsi to make his get-away.

Mrs. Howard Taylor, Hsi's biographer, describes this turbulent time: "For in the midst of these troubles terrible complications arose in other directions also, and from the strangest variety of causes. Disasters occurred in all the leading Refuges, any one of which would have been serious alone. While his enemies prospered, he was compassed with distresses, 'weighed down exceedingly' with a succession of trials such as he had never known before. But as the sufferings abounded, so also was the consolation. In those dark days Hsi was brought to an end of himself and all human resources and learned the deeper meaning of that sentence of death in ourselves that drives us to trust 'not in ourselves, but in God which raiseth the dead.'"

The success of these wicked opposers alarmed and puzzled many of the church-members. Rival Refuges were begun near most of those established by Hsi. Methods were imitated as well as could be done by men whose motives were not right. But some power seemed to grant unexpected success to these imitators who had worked with Hsi long enough to gain a knowledge of his methods and medicine. Hsi had been very successful in preparing medical pills which had greatly alleviated the opium addicts in their struggle for freedom. The formula for these prescriptions had been kept secret by Hsi but now they became open to all and were used by the opponents to try to undo the work of the Lord.

Those who remained true to Hsi had expected immediate judgment to fall on the offenders and traitors. And when, on the contrary, they grew bolder and more prosperous, their plausible reasonings seemed to gain weight. In the following paragraphs, Pastor Hsi reveals to us a little of what he must have endured:

"At that time, the Heavenly Father allowed Satan to buffet me and try me with fire in a manner quite different from anything I had before experienced. There were three false brethren connected with the Refuge work who endeavored to kill me. But, trusting in the Lord, I escaped out of their hands. In four of the leading Refuges there were deaths among those who were breaking off opium, and in all the others we had great and special troubles. And for nearly two years this testing continued.

"Each time I met with heavy trials—all of which I received from the hands of my Heavenly Father—I used to fast for three, four or five days, and the tears that I shed were beyond knowledge. But the Lord opened a way of escape for me. And although I endured much loss of means and weariness and alarm—still, in the end, it was peace. For in the midst of it all, the Lord comforted and strengthened me, and kept me from growing cold-hearted and going back. Now, thanks be to God's grace, all the Refuges are in peace."

Both Hsi and Mr. Host, the leader of the C. I. M. Mission, were convinced that only prayer and patience rather than a great amount of human effort would bring this trouble to an end. The months began to show a crack in the opposition. Hsi again, in a period of prayer and fasting, received this verse, John 15:6, which to him well described a man like Fan: "If a man abide not in me, he is cast forth as a branch, and is withered." He was convinced that this came to him as a direct message from his Heavenly Father, and in all the leading centers he called the attention of the Christians to what he felt was about to happen.

"Rest and quietly wait," he said. "We do not need to fight in this battle. Within three months you will see the last of these spurious Refuges brought to an end." Bold as this statement was, his Heavenly Father did not let his words fall to the ground. One by one, these false Refuges began to fail. Fan lost his influence on his former followers, and becoming involved in hopeless complications, disappeared entirely from the scene.

Another form of opposition Hsi encountered was from honored and respected missionaries who thought they saw perils in the Refuge work. Rumors spread that Hsi was making money through these homes for opium addicts. "From that time," Hsi said, "my strength of heart for work in the Refuges seemed considerably weakened, and the battle was harder to fight. The devil also, using this opportunity disturbed me not a little, suggesting:

"'The task you are attempting is truly an ungrateful one. It is criticized by outsiders and disapproved even by missionaries. It absorbs your money, your time, and your strength. To the end of your days you will never be free from care, or able to obtain rest. You and your wife seldom see each other's faces.'"

The effect of these false rumors continued for ten long years, but this only drove Pastor Hsi to the Lord for the power to "seldom see each other's faces."

Lord, Thou dost put great honor on Thine own,
I thank Thee, I may be
Pained, Lord, for love of Thee.

Accused, misjudged by dearly loved ones here,
I thank Thee, I may be
Blamed, Lord, for love of Thee.

Counted a fool, held up unto contempt,
I thank Thee I may be
Shamed, Lord, for love of Thee.

Lord, I would praise Thee for high privilege,
For pain, and blame and shame,
Suffered for Thy dear Name.

—Stacy Watson

DR. TALMAGE
CALLS BACK

"There was given to me a thorn in the flesh."
2 CORINTHIANS 12:7

ALTHOUGH, down through the centuries, many of God's servants have been obscure, hidden and unnoticed, it has been given to some few to occupy prominent positions in the Church. Lest they become proud, however, a thorn in the flesh has often been given them. De Witt Talmage has been considered by some, the Whitefield of his own times, and his oratory has stirred thousands of his listeners and readers. However, few know of the "malevolent falsehood which hung over the lives of Dr. Talmage and his second wife until the latter passed beyond the knowledge of such things."

Dr. Talmage never used the platform to air his innocency for sixteen years, and then he broke the silence by revealing the truth in a declaration from the pulpit. Here is the exact statement as recorded in Frank Talmage's biography of his father:

"There is a falsehood which strikes a different key, for it strikes the sanctity of my home, and when I tell the story, the fair-minded men and women and children will be indignant. I will read it so that if any one may want to copy it they can.

"It has been stated over and over again in private circles and hinted in newspapers until tens of thousands of people have heard the report, that sixteen or seventeen years ago I went sailing on the Schuylkill River with my wife and her sister, who was my sister-in-law; that the boat capsized, and, having the opportunity of saving either my wife or her sister, I let my wife drown and saved the sister, I, marrying her in sixty days.

"I propose to nail the infamous lie on the forehead of every villain who shall utter it again and to invoke the law to help me."

Dr. Talmage then went on to say that it was his own sister and his young niece who accompanied them that fateful day when they had gone boating. Being newcomers to Philadelphia, none of them knew of the dam further down the river until it was too late to withstand the strong current. The boat overturned, and Mrs. Talmage was sucked under the dam. His own daughter was "nine-tenths dead" but revived after one hour's resuscitation.

"Since the world was created," said Dr. Talmage, "a more ghastly and agonizing calamity never happened. And that is the scene over which some ministers of the Gospel, and men and women pretending to be decent, have made sport."

The woman who became his second wife was not within one hundred miles of the scene, and it was not until some months had passed since the tragedy, that he even met her who was to become his partner. The lies, however, did work some good for Talmage, but we will hear it from his own lips as told in a sermon appearing in *Christian World*:

"I think it was in 1870, and while walking in the park, I found myself asking the question, 'I wonder if there is any special mission for me to execute in this world? If there is, may God show it to me!' There soon came upon me a great desire to preach the Gospel through the secular printing-press. I realized that the vast majority of people, even in Christian lands, never enter a church, and that it would be an opportunity of usefulness infinite if that door of publication were opened.

"And so I recorded that prayer in a blank book, and offered the prayer day in and day out until the answer came, though in a way different from that which I had expected. It came through the misrepresentation and persecution of enemies, and I have to record it for the encouragement of all ministers of the Gospel who are misrepresented, that, if the misrepresentation be virulent enough and bitter enough and continuous enough, there is nothing that so widens one's field of usefulness as hostile attack, if you are really doing the Lord's work. The bigger the lie told about me, the bigger the demand to see and hear what I was really doing....The syndicates inform me that my sermons go now to about 25,000,000 of people in all lands."

Other misfortunes befell this preacher in that three times his tabernacle burned down, the last large edifice catching fire just after he had finished his retirement sermon. He and his wife narrowly escaped before the walls collapsed. Fortunately, the smoldering fire broke out just as the last of thousands of listeners had left the building.

Dr. Talmage, unlike many Presbyterian ministers, did not oppose the cause of holiness. He had a very high estimate of Mrs. Phoebe Palmer, and attended, at one time, her holiness meeting where he rose and expressed his need of this experience. John Boyd in *Divine Life* tells us of this event:

"When the leader of the meeting requested those present who desired the experience of 'perfect love' to stand up, Dr. Talmage was among the first to do so and request prayers of the meeting on his behalf. He said, 'I greatly desire this rich grace that you have been speaking about in such glowing language this afternoon. I feel that my mind and heart are like a machine shop, where every wheel is belted and in motion, save one which stands silent and alone. That wheel is holiness. If it were only like the rest, in motion and at work, I know that I should be equipped for spiritual service as never before. I ask your prayers this afternoon that the Lord, as never before, will put that belt on that motionless wheel, to His own glory and my full and complete salvation."

In a sermon preached later, Talmage exhorted his listeners to believe that their enemies could work out good for them: "I have had multitudes of friends, but I have found in my own experience that

CALL BACK SERIES · VOLUME 1

God so arranged it that the greatest opportunities of usefulness that have been opened before me were opened by enemies. And when, years ago, they conspired against me, that opened all Christendom to me as a field in which to preach the Gospel. So you may harness your antagonists to your best interests, and compel them to draw you on to better work and higher character.

"Oh! It takes these people who have had trouble to comfort others in trouble. Where did Paul get the ink with which to write his comforting epistle? Where did David get the ink to write his comforting Psalms? Where did John get the ink to write his comforting revelation? They got it out of their own tears. When a man has gone through the curriculum, and has taken a course of dungeons and imprisonments and shipwrecks, he is qualified for the work of sympathy.

"When I began to preach, I used to write out all my sermons, and I sometimes have great curiosity to look at the sermons I used to preach on trouble. They were nearly all poetic and in semi-blank verse; but God knocked the blank verse out of me long ago; and I have found out that I cannot comfort people except as I myself have been troubled. God make me the son of consolation to the people."

If you would to another heart a source of comfort be,
Skilled to administer true balm, and show real sympathy:
If you would dry another's tears in deepest grief or woe,
O, marvel not then if today your own heart's blood must flow!

If you would in life's stress and strain, courage and strength impart
To those who 'neath Life's burden oft might droop with sinking heart,—
You, too, must know the pressures keen, the spirit sorely tried,
Draw for yourself the strength from God that never is denied.

Would you equipped for service be, where'er your path may lie?
God has His training school *on Earth*, learn *here* your calling high,—
When pain or joy shall to you come, perceive *His* coming too,
To train you even now for work He has for you to do.

—Ethel Bentnall

JOSEPH ENTWISTLE
CALLS BACK

"I will bring the third part through the fire."
ZECHARIAH 13:9

"Being defamed, we intreat: we are made as the filth of the world, and are the offscouring of all things unto this day."
1 CORINTHIANS 4:13

Sometimes in biographies I think I can see where the Gethsemane is. It may be, and often is, the rooting out of some cherished ambition that has filled the heart and occupied every thought, every dream for years and years. It may be the shattering of some song, the breaking of some dream. It may be, and often is, a great rending of the affections, the cutting the soul free from some detaining, human tenderness. Well, we do not know—the real Gethsemane never lasts long. I think an hour is the longest that anybody could bear it—"Could ye not watch with me one hour?" True, the heartache may go on to the end, but the Gethsemane, that cannot last a long time.

We may be sure that no life will bring forth fruit to God if it is without its Gethsemane, with the great drops of blood in it; and I believe that just as the Savior's blood dropped in Gethsemane and the ground blest it, so the blood of the surrendered soul makes its Gethsemane a garden, if not now, then hereafter; but the time must be, whenever a martyr's blood has been shed, upon that ground the fruits of righteousness must spring.

What is it that should follow when we have parted with our life and lived our Gethsemane; what should be the effect upon our lives? Well, what ought to follow is, that the resurrection life, which the shedding of blood has made room for, should take the place of the other.—J. H. Jowett

Christ of the dreadful Gethsemane,
Facing that infamous tragedy,
Bearing in spirit the world's great crime,
We'll not forget ere the end of time.
Bowing in anguish, we share with Thee
Testing, triumphant Gethsemane.

—Unknown

Recently, when reading the autobiography of Joseph Entwistle, we recognized the Gethsemane that this very godly Methodist preacher in England passed through, and we were greatly inspired and moved.

It might be said of him that he prayed to God always, and he entered into a very vital experience of total commitment, resulting in heart-cleansing. He married the niece of a very prominent Methodist family, known as the Mathers and noted for their godliness.

Entwistle was of a very warm-hearted nature and enjoyed very close fellowship with a most apparently sincere and earnest young friend. A friendship seemed forged in the Lord that would last a life-time. They confided in each other and enjoyed reading the Bible and praying together; together they went into the house of the Lord.

And then a terrible blow was stuck by this young man—so totally unexpected as to leave Entwistle dazed. First he became very bitter against Mr. Entwistle's brother, and then turned also upon his former friend. He seemed determined to ruin him.

He accused the broken-hearted confidant of former days of owing him a considerable debt which he had refused to pay. He threatened the minister with court action and was so persistent that daily the innocent Christian dreaded the sound of a knock at his door lest it be that of an officer of the court who would serve a summons. Night and day Satan troubled him as to how it would turn out. His detractor spread the slander from door-to-door in the village amidst the parishioners who listened to the accuser.

One Sunday, Joseph Entwistle, with an aching heart, told the congregation of his intense suffering and protested his innocence of the charge. It seemed the only course he could take if he remained among his people as a minister of God's Word. The whole affair was committed to God, and the preacher came to enjoy a closer walk with Him.

After a year came the startling news that his betrayer was in serious trouble with the police in Manchester. He had been accused of stealing a considerable quantity of cloth from a warehouse and faced transportation or even capital punishment which was not uncommon in those days. The preacher had been at last vindicated, and suspicion and gossip died away.

There will be no Christian but will have a Gethsemane; but every Christian will find that there is no Gethsemane without its angel!

—T. Bubbet

> All those who journey, soon or late,
> Must pass within the garden's gate;
> Must kneel alone in darkness there,
> And battle with some fierce despair.
> God pity those who cannot say,
> "Not mine but Thine"; who only pray
> "Let this cup pass," and cannot see
> The purpose in Gethsemane.
>
> —E. W. Wilcox

RICHARD WEAVER AND HENRY SUSO CALL BACK

"I was a reproach among all mine enemies, but especially among my neighbors, and a fear to mine acquaintance: they that did see me without fled from me. I am forgotten as a dead man out of mind: I am like a broken vessel. For I have heard the slander of many."

PSALMS 31:11-13

RICHARD WEAVER had had a remarkable conversion and then was called to evangelistic labors. His indefatigable zeal and originality won for him a place in the estimation of the British public. Throughout the British Isles, his services were in demand for series after series of ministering labors. Then rumors spread about some immoral conduct and this was so universally accepted as truth, that for a year, Weaver was isolated and rejected. Public condemnation caused appointments to cease and platforms previously so open to him were now closed. One Glasgow minister, however, of considerable influence, at last convinced of his innocence, opened the doors of his tabernacle to the wounded and rejected evangelist.

No misunderstanding can be so difficult to a man used of God as that which blights his moral character. The godly monk and poet whose poems still speak to the heart also faced this fiery ordeal. Henry Suso had been highly revered in his own neighborhood as a pious man. People sought his counsel daily until...one morning, upon opening his front door, he was surprised to discover a strange bundle on his doorstep—a tiny baby not many days old! A note accompanied the newly born infant, accusing Suso of being the father of the child.

The man of God took the infant into his own dwelling, and after some conflict of mind, felt God willed him to welcome heartily and to oversee the care of the unwanted child. He offered no explanations to inquisitive neighbors; he made no protests of innocency. By some spiritual intuitiveness, Henry Suso was made to understand that God would one day reveal to him the purpose of this strange and unexpected trial.

Doubtless to the onlooker, his conduct but seemed to justify suspicions, and town gossips must have chewed over such a juicy morsel—"Imagine such a man of integrity and spotless character being so caught out!"

For a year the child was cared for. But one day vindication of his character came swiftly. The mother of the child lay upon her death bed, and filled with horror for her deceitfulness, confessed that she had plotted the whole affair at the instigation of a priest who hated the godly Suso. So after the weary procession of 365 days and nights with the shadow of immoral conduct hanging over him, the man of God came forth to labor more effectually for his Master.

That suffering had done a refining work on the poet is manifest in his beautiful poems, one of which is entitled, "The Door Mat."

"It was winter morning in the days of old,
In his cell sat Father Henry, sorrowful and cold.
'O my Lord, I am weary,' in his heart he spake,
'For my brethren scorn and hate me for Thy blessed sake.

"'If I had but one to love me, that were joyful cheer—
One small word to make me sunshine through the darksome year!
But they mock me and despise me till my heart is stung—
Then my words are wild and bitter, tameless is my tongue.'

"Then the Lord said, 'I am with thee; trust thyself to Me;
Open thou thy little casement; mark what thou shalt see.'
Then a piteous look and wistful Father Henry cast
Out into the dim, old cloister and the wintry blast.

"Was it that a friend was coming by some angel led?
No! A great hound, wild and savage round the cloister sped.

169

Some old mat that lay forgotten seized he on his way—
Tore it, tossed it, dragged it wildly round the cloister gray.

"'Lo, the hound is like thy brethren,' spake the Voice he knew;
'If thou art the mat, beloved, what has thou to do?'
Meekly then went Father Henry and the mat he bear
To his little cell, to store it as jewel rare.

"Many a winter and a summer through those cloisters dim
Did he thenceforth walk rejoicing and the Lord with him.
And when bitter words would sting him, turned he to his cell,
Took his mat, and looked upon it saying, 'All is well.

"'He who is the least and lowest needs but low to lie;
Lord, I thank Thee and I praise Thee that the mat am I.'
Then he wept for in the stillness his beloved spake,
'Thus was I the least and lowest, gladly for thy sake.
Lo, My face to shame and spitting did I turn for thee;
If thou art the least and lowest then remember Me.'"

DAVID AND MARY LIVINGSTONE CALL BACK

"They wandered in the wilderness in a solitary way; they found no city to dwell in. ....He led them forth by the right way, that they might go to a city of habitation."

PSALMS 107:4, 7

THE BOAT ROCKED slightly in the breeze on the Zambesi as night settled down on David and Mary Livingstone. Night sounds which only are heard in tropical Africa were floating in on the quiet of that evening. In the flickering light one could see Mary Livingstone on an improvised bed made up of a soft mattress set on boxes. It was evident to Dr. Stewart and David who stood by, that the end was not far off. David was overcome with grief. He, who could face a thousand dangers, now stood crumpled before this formidable parting.

After a separation of nearly four years in which each had suffered "almost to the limit of human endurance," they had been re-united. The following poem, written by Mary, expresses how costly was her loneliness:

> A hundred thousand welcomes! How my heart is gushing o'er
> With the love and joy and wonder thus to see your face once more.
> How did I live without you these long, long years of woe?
> It seems as if 'twould kill me to be parted from you now.
>
> Do you think I would reproach you with the sorrow that I bore
> Since the sorrow is all over, now I have you here once more?
> And there's nothing but the gladness and the love within my heart,
> And the hope so sweet and certain that again we'll never part.

After so long a time apart, Mary had anticipated the joy of being with David in his journeys. She had brought household items with her with which to brighten their new home. Together they went through the packing boxes and David was in ecstasies, so much so that he chided himself for such joy. But they were to be granted only three short months in one another's company. "The main spoke in his wheel" as he had described his Mary, was to be taken. The fever-laden air of the swamps had been too much for her. Unable to take his boat, *The Pioneer*, upstream because of low water and many sandbanks, David could do little to save his beloved wife.

"O my Mary, my Mary," he wrote in his journal after her death. "How often we have longed for a quiet home, since you and I were cast adrift at Kolobeng; surely this removal by a kind Father Who knoweth our frames means that He rewarded you by taking you to the best Home, the eternal one in the Heavens."

It was not that David had failed to provide that quiet home. He had built one for his young bride at Mabotsa where the work among the heathen seemed to be making considerable headway. With thoughtful, loving hands he had planted a garden with trees that would ensure produce for years to come. But this quiet home was to be denied them.

Bitter and painful were the recollections of that collision which had taken place with the senior missionary at Mabotsa. Accusations had multiplied discrediting David as a "non-entity" to missionaries and directors at home. The older missionary "refused to be made an appendix to a younger man." David's daring irked his colleague, proving an unhappy contrast to the latter's humdrum, missionary endeavors. In order to prevent friction on the station which might well have proved a stumbling-block to the converts, the Livingstones made a supreme sacrifice—to go and start anew elsewhere.

Livingstone felt this situation acutely and, in his letters written during this time, there is a "tone of indignation that after having carried the heat and burden of the day he should be accused of claiming for himself the credit due to one who had done so little in comparison."

He would not have minded leaving his garden to one who would have tenderly cared for it, but to know it would be left to "tasteless hands" to become once again a wilderness was too much. "I like a garden," he wrote, "but paradise will make amends for all our privations and sorrows here." Mabotsa did not thrive after the departure of the Livingstones.

Together the young couple started afresh with scarcely any money in hand with which to buy materials. Applying to the Mission Board for a building grant, they found there were those who would object to the sum of only thirty pounds. So they tightened their belts and lived frugally. "We endured for a long while," wrote David, "using a wretched infusion of native corn for coffee, but when our corn was done, we were fairly obliged to go to Kuruman for supplies. I can bear what other Europeans would consider hunger and thirst without inconvenience, but when we arrived, to hear the old woman, who had seen my wife depart about two years before, exclaiming, 'Bless me! How lean she is! Has he starved her? Is there no food in the country to which she has been?' was more than I could bear."

But Mary's spirit was indomitable, too. In a letter she wrote: "Let others plead for pensions. I can be rich without money; I could give my services in the world from disinterested motives; I have motives for my own conduct I would not exchange for a hundred pensions."

Mary's heart was torn between the best for her children who needed to be educated back in Scotland, and her deep desire to be with her husband whose strength she needed to feel at times of decision making. The desire for a comfortable home was denied her even in her stay in Scotland, for though many friends were kind, it was not a happy time for the mother and children. Her desire to go back and rear a home for her husband in Africa became so strong that she returned with furnishings in her trunk for that longed-for place.

For three months she was with her husband traveling as usual. And when fever and sickness impaired her natural spirit, she spoke despondingly to David stating that she would never again find a "home" in Africa. Had he only known she was so ill he would have talked it all out with his partner, but he had only thought it was her morbid way of thinking due to illness. To a friend shortly after her death he confided, "A brave, good woman was she. All my hopes of giving her one day a quiet home for which we both had many a sore longing, are now dashed to the ground. She is, I trust, through divine mercy, in peace in the home of the blest."

Perhaps, however, that which was hardest of all to bear, had been the harassment of scandal-mongers who hinted that, because of their frequent partings, things were not stable in the Livingstones' marriage relationship. A doctor of divinity had been heard to remark once regarding Mary: "Oh, she is no good; she is here because her husband cannot live with her." Even more hurtful were the intimations, equally false, that David, following the example of many white men alone in the African bush, had had illicit relationships with various native women.

These malicious rumors caused the slandered missionary to write thus: "I regret, as there always are regrets after our loved ones are gone, that the slander which, unfortunately, reached her ears from missionary gossips and others, had an influence on me in allowing her to come, before we were fairly on Lake Nyasa." He refers here to those last months Mary spent with him among the swamps at the mouth of the Zambesi.

Mrs. Moffat, Mary's mother, in a letter to David, exonerates the two: "As for the cruel slander that seems to have hurt you both so much, those who said it did not know you as a couple. In all our intercourse with you, we never had a doubt as to your being comfortable together. I know there are some maudlin ladies who insinuate when a man leaves his family frequently, no matter how noble is his object, that he is not comfortable at home. But we can afford to smile at this, and say, 'The Day will declare it.'"

God never, never shields from all suffering those He designs to train for service in His future Kingdom. But neither does He allow them to sink into oblivion. Those who spread the scandal and caused the misrepresentations have been forgotten. Their names are not known to us, but "they that be wise and turn many to righteousness shall be as the stars that shine forever in the firmament."

Then came the last day of moving for the lone, suffering traveler. God granted him his desire as to his last resting place: "I have often wished that it might be in some far-off, still, deep forest, where I may sleep sweetly till the resurrection morn." David was found by his two faithful servants on his knees beside his cot. Moving days were ended. No more traveling! No more weary marches, fever, and threat of danger. No more striking camp and folding up the tents for still another journey. The last enemy had been conquered; the last move had been made and now—"Home forever."

> Earth gave Thee a cradle,
> O Christ, and a cross,
> Hard roads for Thy journey,
> Reviling and loss;
> Earth gave Thee Thy wounding,
> Thy shroud and Thy tomb,
> But earth gave no welcome
> And earth gave no home.
>
> —Sel.

HANDEL
CALLS BACK

*"He is despised and rejected of men; a man of sorrows, and
acquainted with grief: and we hid as it were our faces from him; he
was despised, and we esteemed him not."*

ISAIAH 53:3

"DESPISED and rejected!" Yes, that description exactly expressed the
melancholy mood of the sixty-year-old bachelor as he dragged his
weary frame through the streets of London, vainly hoping to banish
boredom and stark discouragement. The dejected man felt so alone in
the heart of that throbbing and teeming population. The London that
had once cheered his successes now had left him alone.

Had he not reason for depressing thoughts when his creditors
were threatening legal action if debts were not promptly paid? His
crippled hands, the unsure step, the slower brain responses—all were
constant reminders of that paralyzing stroke which had threatened
his brilliant career. If in all these trials, he had had a cheerful, wifely
companion to share his misfortunes, or even the loving solicitude of
parents or countrymen, George Frederick Handel would not have felt
so desperately forsaken and forlorn.

He had known balmier days when packed London audiences
waited breathlessly to hear his performances on the organ of his own
Italian operatic compositions. The nobility and even royalty itself had
opened their palatial dwellings for the German musician, but now the
fickle crowd had become absorbed with some other passing meteor
and had turned their backs on him. Rejected—yes, he was realizing to
the full the meaning, and it penetrated him through and through.

Now he was nearing in his rambles the dull, gray edifice of a
church, and bitter and anguished thoughts welled up within him:

"Why did God permit my resurrection only to allow my fellow-men to bury me again? Why did He vouchsafe a renewal of my life if I may no longer be permitted to create?" And then, as though anticipating the future creation of his "Messiah," his heart fellowshipped with the dying Jesus as he groaned out spontaneously, "My God, my God, why hast thou forsaken me?" Rejected—surely there was some friend somewhere into whose sympathetic ears he could pour out the bitterness, isolation, and despondency into which his present sense of fading powers had plunged him.

Reaching his abode, and he mounted the steps slowly and with leaden feet. Lighting the candles, Handel noticed a bulky packet had been placed upon his desk in his absence. Opening the parcel, he noted that it was from Charles Jenne, a "foppish aristocrat" who had arranged some Scripture verses for Handel to set to music.

But seating himself, the composer slowly read over the Bible description of a suffering Messiah. "He was despised and rejected of men,...and we hid as it were our faces from him." Here was Someone Who had passed the same way. Suddenly a glow of inspiration suffused his inactive brain. It leaped into action. The heavens were opened and Handel saw into the invisible realm. Heavenly organ strains floated unbidden through his whole being. He reached for his pen and the crippled fingers worked feverishly. "He trusted God...he will give you rest." The words became alive. "Wonderful, Counselor, I know that my Redeemer liveth...Rejoice...Hallelujah!"

The depression had lifted. The melodious harmonies of mighty choruses rose and swelled as music for orchestra, organ, and voice deluged the once barren mind of the composer.

All night Handel wrote the notes lest he forget. The next morning, the tray of food for breakfast was set beside him, but what was food! The creative urge was there and the muse was working. Nothing must erase the chords that were chasing each other through his quickened sensibilities.

For twenty-four days, the inspired German worked almost non-stop, but at last the oratorio in three parts, "The Messiah," was completed. Exhausted, the creator of music lay down to rest and for seventeen hours seemed as if in a coma.

"A miracle lifted me from the deepest despondency. Now let it be the hope of the world," were the words of the renewed artist. Then came an invitation from the Lord Lieutenant of Ireland to perform in Dublin. Seven hundred pressed into the hall usually only holding six hundred. Handel's performance had been a success. But London was not to respond so quickly. It has been said that if one is acceptable to Londoners, he is made in the world. But even when Handel made an attempt to come back in 1743, the three efforts were abortive. Street urchins were paid to tear down the posters announcing his concerts and society women planned pleasurable events to coincide with his performances to draw off the crowds from his "Messiah." Another two performances were attempted in 1745 and still London remained unmoved.

It had been nine years since that August night, when he had suddenly experienced that miracle of a revelation which had lifted him out of the deepest despondency. Nine years are a very long time when you hope to share something good with the public who has misrepresented and misunderstood you. But God is never in a hurry, for as Alexander Whyte remarked, "We cease to wonder so much at the care God takes of human character, and the cost He lays out upon it, when we think that it is the only work of His hands that shall last forever. It is fit, surely, that the ephemeral should minister to the eternal and time to eternity, and all else in this world to the only thing in the world that shall endure and survive this world. All else we possess and pursue shall fade and perish; our moral character shall alone survive. Riches, honors, possessions, pleasures of all kinds—death, with one stroke of his desolating hand shall one day strip us bare in a winding-sheet and a coffin of all things we are so mad to possess."

London finally accepted the formerly rejected composer. "Handel," said Lord Kinnoul, "you have provided a noble entertainment for the town."

Handel replied, "My Lord, I should be sorry to think it was only an entertainment. I intended it should make them better." And because he knew the work was not his but Another's, he gave all the proceeds to charity.

Everything that continues to bless mankind has come out of the crucible of human suffering. It is a world of broken hearts, and no author, musician, poet, or speaker, who has not had his life burned to white heat in the flame of some great disappointment or sorrow, can write so as to touch another's heart.

No—you may call and call me, but I have no time to hear you,
For I have heard a stranger call to something high and far.
Illume your night with fireworks, flash the trinkets that can cheer you—
No glimmer stabs my dark—but in my midnight gleams a star!

I have no time to listen to the light wind of your chatter.
The swish of whirling worlds takes bated breath and straining ears.
And while you're dripping platitudes, and while your teacups clatter,
I might squander in a minute the long vigilance of years.

You have no key to comprehend the magic that enthralls me.
He who would sound the depths of it counts all things else as toys.
To your ears never penetrates the driving voice that calls me,
Nor to your hearts the pure white fire of a discoverer's joys!

—Gladys Batte

A. B. SIMPSON
CALLS BACK

"But God hath chosen the foolish things of the world to confound the wise; and God hath chosen the weak things of the world to confound the things which are mighty: And base things of the world, and things which are despised, hath God chosen, yea, and things which are not, to bring to nought things that are."

1 CORINTHIANS 1:27-28

"**No MAN** has ever attained supreme knowledge unless his heart has been torn up by the roots," said Francis Thompson, author of *The Hound of Heaven*. And that saintly Christian, Robert Chapman, must likewise have learned the same secret when he said, "When Christ would put peculiar honor upon His servants, He often suffers them to be brought low in the sight of men. If the saints are favored to suffer reproach for Christ's sake, then will they own the honor put upon them to be thus conformed to their Master. Paul and Silas, thrust into prison at Philippi, sang praises to God. Christ never allows any faithful servants of His to suffer loss but He turns that loss to great gain. God always honors faithful servants and comforts persecuted ones."

> "Whether man's heart or life it be which yields
> Thee harvest, must Thy harvest-fields
> Be dunged with rotten death?"
>
> —Francis Thompson

Gregory Mantle in his book, *Beyond Humiliation*, cites the experience of two ministers of the Gospel who experienced what it was to be utterly rejected of their fellow-men.

"One of my intimate, ministerial friends had an experience which has suggested the title of this chapter, 'The Pathway of Rejection.' His congregation persistently refused to accept his message. He wanted to lead his flock into green pastures and beside the still waters, but they were unwilling to be led. His choir, with their ungodly practices, brought things to a crisis.

"The position had become so unbearable that he invited the choir to resign, for he felt like one of old—whenever he attempted to preach, that 'Satan stood at his right hand to resist him.' The choir not only resigned but persuaded the congregation to desist from taking any part in the singing.

"The result was that whatever singing was done had to be done by the preacher, the choir and congregation rejoicing in his discomfiture, and refusing to join. This state of things continued for some time, and quite naturally, my friend was greatly dejected and perplexed at the turn events had taken. He was at his wits' end when God spoke to him. He was sitting one day on a seat in a park when he saw before him on the ground part of a torn newspaper. That torn paper had a message for him that exactly suited his need. It was this:

> "'No man is ever fully accepted until he has, first
> of all, been utterly rejected.'

"He needed nothing more. He had been utterly rejected, and his recognition of the fact was the beginning of a most fruitful ministry in another sphere which continues to this day, and proves how fully he had been accepted by God though so utterly rejected by man.

"It was so with Dr. A. B. Simpson of New York, the founder of the Christian and Missionary Alliance.

"This is how Dr. Simpson himself describes the second of these crises: 'I look back with unutterable gratitude to the lonely and sorrowful night when mistaken in many things and imperfect in all, and not knowing but that it would be death in the most literal sense before the morning light, my heart's first full consecration was made, and with unreserved surrender I first could say:

> 'Jesus, I my cross have taken,
> All to leave and follow Thee,
> Destitute, despised, forsaken,
> Thou from hence, my all shalt be.'

"'Never perhaps, has my heart known quite such a thrill of joy as when the following Sabbath morning I gave out those lines and sang them with all my heart.'

"Dr. Simpson had to learn later, when in response to the call of God he resigned his pastorate, what it really meant to be 'destitute, despised, forsaken.' He surrendered a (then) lucrative salary, a position as a leading pastor in the greatest American city and all claim upon his denomination for assistance in a yet untried work. He was in a great city with no following, no organization, no financial resources, with a large family dependent upon him, and with his most intimate, ministerial friends and former associates predicting failure. So completely was he misunderstood, even by those from whom he expected sympathy, that he once said he often looked down upon the paving stones in the streets for the sympathy that was denied him elsewhere.

"The rugged path of utter rejection was trodden not only uncomplainingly but with rejoicing. He knew that though he was brought into the net and was going through fire and water, it was the divinely appointed way to the wealthy place. He reached the wealthy place at last; and in a sense, beyond his wildest dreams, he found himself fully accepted by God. Think of his monument! Schools for the training of missionaries; missionaries and native evangelists in many lands; not a few heroic pioneers occupying strategic positions in the most distant missionary outposts; a prolific and anointed pen, always pouring forth heart-searching sermons; the creation of the highest type of literature 'whereby he being dead yet speaketh'; and best of all, the multitude who greeted him and will yet greet him on the other shore, turned from sin to righteousness through his instrumentality.

"What an illustration of the pathway of rejection! Scores of illustrations of this great principle might be given, beginning with Christ, the most illustrious. 'He was despised and rejected of men.'"

—Beyond Humiliation

The words of A. B. Simpson, taken from his book, *Power from on High*, assume a new authority when we realize how qualified the author was to write them, due to his personal encounter with rejection:

"The Lord still is using the things that are despised. The very names of Nazarene and Christian were once epithets of contempt. No man can have God's highest thought and be popular with his immediate generation. The most abused men are often the most used. The devil's growl and the world's sneer are God's marks of highest honor. There is no need that we should bring upon ourselves by folly or wrong the reproaches of men, but if we do well and suffer for it, fear not but 'let Shimei curse, the Lord will requite us good for his cursing this day.'

"There are far greater calamities than to be unpopular and misunderstood. There are far worse things than to be found in the minority. Many of God's greatest blessings are lying behind the devil's scarecrows of prejudice and misrepresentation. The Holy Ghost is not ashamed to use unpopular people. And if He uses them, why need they care for men?

"There was once a captain in the British army promoted for merit, but despised by his aristocratic companions. One day, the Colonel found it out and determined to stop it. So he quietly called on the young officer and walked arm in arm with him up and down the parade ground, the captains meanwhile being obliged to salute both him and his companion, every time they passed. That settled the new captain's standing. After that, there were no cuts or sneers. It was enough that the commanding officer had walked by his side.

"Oh, let us but have His recognition and man's notice will count for little, and He will give us all we need of human help and praise.

Let us make no compromise to please men. Let us only seek His will, His glory, His approval. Let us go for Him on the hardest errands and do the most menial tasks. Honor enough that He uses us and sends us. Let us not fear in this day to follow Him outside the camp, bearing His reproach, and bye-and-bye He will own our worthless name before the myriads of earth and sky."

MAURICE REUBEN
CALLS BACK

*"But rejoice, inasmuch as ye are partakers of
Christ's sufferings; that, when his glory shall be revealed,
ye may be glad also with exceeding joy"*

1 PETER 4:13

MAURICE REUBEN belonged to a wealthy family, had the best the world could give him and lived to make money. He was director of Solomon and Reuben, one of the largest stores in Pittsburgh. However, the life of one of his buyers used to put him under deep conviction, until one day he said to him, "You must have been born happy."

"Yes," replied the buyer, "in my second birth. I accepted the Lord Jesus Christ and was born of God. In my first birth I was no happier than you!"

Reuben was so moved by this testimony that he bought a New Testament, and there he was impressed with the fact that all those who followed Jesus were Jews; John the Baptist pointing to Him as the Lamb of God; Peter, James and John, the chief disciples; and to a Jew the Savior had said, "On this rock I will build my Church." Then he came to the story of the rich young ruler. It was a dramatic moment—a rich Jew of the twentieth century and under conviction, reading of the Savior's dealings with a rich Jew of the first century! The way that Reuben saw it was that if Jesus had told that young man to sell all to inherit eternal life, how could he, Reuben, inherit the same gift, unless on the same condition? It was his supreme test. If he became a disciple, he knew that he, too, stood to lose all. But it was too late to go back; he had seen it, and he must follow.

Reuben faced it fairly and squarely and counted the cost. His wife might leave him, his brother put him out of the business, and not a single Jew follow him, but he had made up his mind; if he lost everything, he meant to do it. Then one day, on the way to the store, Reuben heard a voice repeating to him the words of John 14:6: "I am the way, the truth, and the life: no man cometh unto the father, but by me." The truth flashed upon him—he accepted Christ and entered into life that moment. He then told his brother and others. According to his father's will, he was to forfeit every penny if he changed his religion, but his brother offered to give him his share of the business if he would cross U.S.A. and retire in Montana. But Reuben replied: "I have had the light in Pittsburgh, and I am going to witness in Pittsburgh."

Late that Saturday night, detectives came and took him to the police station. On Monday, two doctors visited his cell and asked him about the voice he had heard. "Do they question my sanity?" he thought. Two hours later, warders came from the asylum and took him to a room where there were twenty-nine mentally deranged people. The bitterness of his position overcame him. He had victory in the lock-up, but this seemed more than he could bear. He fell on his knees by his bed and poured out his heart to the Lord. He did not know how long he was there, but he seemed to lose himself, and a vision of Calvary appeared to him. He said he witnessed every stage of the crucifixion. He forgot his own sufferings in the sufferings of the Savior, and as he gazed on the Cross, the Master Himself said to him, "And must I bear the Cross alone, and all the world go free?" From a broken heart Reuben answered, "No. There's a cross for everyone, and there's a cross for me." From that hour he was a new man. Instead of complaining at being in the asylum, he began to pray for the other twenty-nine inmates, and to the Savior he said: "Let me suffer for You. Whatever You allow me to go through, I will never complain again."

Two weeks later, Reuben's brother came to see him and reproached him for his folly in getting himself into such a place. "Why won't you be wise?" he asked. "Get out of here and go to Montana." "Does that offer still stand? Then it is not a medical condition but something else that is keeping me here!" concluded Reuben with all the keenness of his logical mind.

Some Christian friends he was in touch with caused inquiries to be set on foot. In six weeks, his release was procured. However, as a result, Rueben became involved in a court case which focused on "the voice" he had heard. The judge called the doctor and asked why this man had been certified insane. "Because he heard a voice," said the doctor.

"Didn't the Apostle Paul hear a voice?" countered the judge, who was a Christian man. "This is a disgrace to the American flag," and he told Reuben to prosecute everyone who had anything to do with it.

"I shall never prosecute one," answered Reuben, "but I will do one thing—I will pray for them." He crossed the court and offered his hand to his brother, but he turned his back on him. He went to his wife, but she did the same. But what a victory he had in his own soul!

He rented a small room in Chicago, where he lived alone with the Lord and won many converts, though for two years he hardly ever had a square meal. A year later, his wife came to hear him in a camp-meeting and was converted, and for the first time, he saw his little boy who had been born after his wife had left him. She was willing to make her home with him again, if only he would earn a living as other Christians did.

His heart went out to his little boy, and this test was even greater than the first. Her request seemed so reasonable, but he knew that the Lord had called him from the world into this life of faith. He pleaded with the Lord, but the only reply he received was, "Back to Egypt!" It was enough, and once more Reuben embraced the Cross. He went to see his wife and child off; it was a costly experience, but as the train steamed out of the station, it seemed that God poured the joy of Heaven into his soul. He literally danced on the platform.

He did not see his wife for another three years. Then, in another camp meeting, she, too, had a revelation of the Cross, as a result of which she testified that, whereas before as a believer she had not been willing to share the sacrificial life of her husband, if it would be for God's glory, she would now be willing to beg her bread from door to door. They were reunited and she became a wonderful co-worker with him in his ministry.

> I'll hide my heart where the white stars burn
>   And the clean winds sweep the sky
> That none may seek it out or learn
>   Of the dreams that whisper by.
>
> For the great souls choose the lonely way,
>   Though tears are dew mist there,
> And the fierce white light of the searching day
>   Lays the scars of the seared heart bare.
>
> Oh, lone and stark the white way streams
>   Like the lash of a scourging rod;
> But the stars are there and those whispering dreams—
>   Aye, and the heart of God.
>
> —Unknown

J. Gordon observes: "I have been struck in observing the various attempts to explain a certain phrase that Paul uses: 'In all these things we are more than conquerors.' Yet how simple it is when taken in its connection. He sums up all the things he is enduring—the sword, peril, nakedness, dying all the day long for Christ, led daily like a sheep to the slaughter; and then he says: 'In all these things we are more than conquerors.' How? Plainly thus: the man who is victorious through victory is a conqueror; but he who is victorious through defeat is more than conqueror."

MARY WARBURTON BOOTH CALLS BACK

"Our God...is able...But if not...we will not serve thy gods"

DANIEL 3:17-18

"GENTLEMEN, when you are face to face with a difficulty, you are up against a discovery," said Lord Kelvin while lecturing to his students after an experiment he was trying had failed. This truth is exemplified in the history of diamond mining when it seemed that the prospectors had reached the end of their successful findings in the yellow soil. Read how this difficulty was overcome:

"In Kimberley's history of diamond exploration, the diggers struck 'blue earth' at a depth of seventy feet. The lovely, yellow soil that had yielded such costly gems was expended, so they thought. Many miners packed up and moved off, and the days of Kimberley mining seemed to have had 'finis' written over it. The bulk of the miners took it for granted that the soil was too hard and unyielding for gems.

"But one man, Dr. Atherstone, reasoned differently. He believed the blue ground worth digging into. It readily yielded to the picks of the diggers and even became like the yellow soil above when exposed to the atmosphere. Then a crystal was discovered and many who had deserted the field returned, rushing back to capitalize in what had been considered worthless. It was a pipe of diamondiferous soil, ten acres wide and almost bottomless."

Mary Warburton Booth's mining was of a different sort. She dealt in the field of human diamonds. Full of zest and zeal for the Lord, she left all her English friends and relatives for her new life-calling in India, and went to work for the Lord of the mines, first in language study and then out among the people. The work was unceasing—schools, zenanas, teaching, and preaching.

"I never worked so hard in my life as I did those five and a half years," she declared, "yet there was so little to show for it. I was heart-sick and weary and down very low when I left India for my furlough, and I hoped against hope that God would never ask me to return to Gorakhpur. The deadness of the so-called Christians, the fruitlessness of the work, the long, long sowing and no reaping were enough to kill any enthusiasm that is not fixed in God."

On her furlough, Miss Booth attended the Keswick Convention and sitting under the preaching one day, she was arrested by the Holy Ghost. The subject was: "But if not . . ." taken from the response of the three Hebrew children to the king when about to be thrown into the fiery furnace.

"You have come to Keswick disappointed because of the way," the preacher was saying. "You have prayed for a revival and nothing has happened and you are thinking: 'The God Whom we serve is able—but—but—but if not?'—what is your answer?

"Will you go back to the old life? You have prayed for revival. Our God Whom we serve is able—but if not—but if not—but if not—" he repeated.

Miss Booth simply records: "I laid my choice in the dust, and knelt at the Cross to pray anew: 'Create in me a clean heart and renew a right spirit within me.'"

Years later, looking back over this period, she writes:

"If only someone had told us, if only we had been taught to wait on the Lord, if only someone had said: 'You must learn to tarry.' We are so eager to be on the move, there is no stillness about us and although we bring the glad tidings of peace, we don't know very much about it."

A few months later she was back at Gorakhpur. "Somehow," she says, "I expected to find things different, but there was no change— the people were the same and there was no change in the atmosphere."

BOOK 3 · FRUSTRATION

"But if not" rang in her ears, and she asked, "What is it, Lord? Where can I find the sheep that is lost?" And He answered, "Ask of Me."

"It took some time," says Miss Booth, "for me to grasp that I needed to give more time for asking in prayer. The hindrances to prayer in India are legion. Satan has every device ready to keep you from praying through. The calls are imperative; the climate exhausting; and the insect life so collective that you are reminded always that you have a body and mosquitoes love you and insects visit you, and they do hinder concentrated prayer ...."

"I was a dazed early riser who could sleep better than pray, and I was so unsuccessful that I dropped it to face things in the day. 'What was the good of it?' I questioned myself, and it came to this: I was really getting up to meet Him. It was a wonderful revelation to me, and when I got up He was there to meet me.

"...And there I knelt in His presence until my being was filled with awe, and I stayed to worship, and from that day I realized that prayer must be the fundamental part of my life: it could no longer be supplemental to what I did, and I began to rise before the dawn just to meet Him. He is not a disappointment. He taught me how to pray and how to wait before Him. The Scriptures opened out priceless treasures, and I soon learned that real prayer is vital in its working. It wasn't long before I discovered that it takes time to know God....Prayer changes things and it changes people, too, and all my life has been transfigured by the habit of prayer, cultivated, persevered, and pursued.

> "Yes, Jesus came, He came to me,
>   Down from His home above,
> And breathed into my longing soul
>   His life, His light, His love.
> He took the disappointment there
>   And turned it into praise.
> And now He walks and talks with me
>   And stays with me always.

191

No darkness falls upon my soul,
I walk with Him in light:
He gave me love, He poured in life,
He answered in the night.

"When God called me to be a missionary I never dreamt of such love; I had no idea of the wonders before me, or of the glory I should see, but every promise He made to me has been fulfilled. He has increased my joy in the Lord and given to me the unspeakable bliss of belonging entirely to Him. The passing years have increased His preciousness to me, and I know that it is better on before, because He is there."

GEORGE PILKINGTON CALLS BACK

"Then I said, I have labored in vain, I have spent my strength for nought, and in vain: yet surely my judgment is with the Lord, and my work with my God."

ISAIAH 49:4

GEORGE PILKINGTON was obviously discouraged. He had been absenting himself of late from the prayer meetings held among the missionaries, and had even spoken of giving up the work altogether unless something transpired to alter the terrible dearth in spiritual results so woefully apparent. Many onlookers would have said his three years on the field should have given him no cause for distress, for he had done some brilliant work in translating the Bible into the language of the Waganda, and the native response for Bibles and books was so overwhelmingly enthusiastic that there was cause for partial gratification. But where was the power to work those "greater works" which Christ had promised? In this state of agitation, George Pilkington went away to the island of Kome for quiet.

To better understand the subject of this sketch, let us look back into his early life and spiritual experience. George Pilkington was born in Dublin, June 4, 1865, of Protestant parents who were staunch Church people. How carefully the mother chose the school where high educational standards and religious and character-molding influences were to be combined. Several scholarships were won, and a Good Conduct Medal was received by George with the inscription, "For good work and unblemished conduct." Said the House-Master at the end of this boy's public school career, "His consistent stand on the side of right can never be blotted out."

Strange currents had been set in motion at Cambridge just two years previous to George's entrance, by the coming of Moody and Sankey. The visit of the "Cambridge Seven" likewise gave fresh impetus to the missionary spirit. Four young men, evangelistically minded and later nicknamed in the College, "The Four Apostles," entered Pembroke College, Cambridge, the same year as George Pilkington. This quartet had a heart-enthusiasm for Christ, and so they divided the fifty-two freshmen between the four of them and visited every man in his room until they had had some direct conversation with him on spiritual matters. Pilkington's first reaction was that Klein and his helpers were mad, and after attending one of their services he stayed behind to prove to them they were preaching nonsense.

But the "four" were nothing daunted, and, eagerly watching for every opportunity of witnessing, they took advantage of a College Debating Society meeting where any man could air his hobby. Klein saw in this a chance to get Christ's message to men who would never attend religious services. Amidst a din, he arose and spoke for ten minutes on the "Life of Faith." Instead of scolding the unconverted, he showed that the lukewarm half-heartedness of the professed followers right there in that room was nothing but hollow insincerity. Sinners were more sincere in that they threw their heart into what they thought was right, while professors of religion lived a lie to the truths they claimed to believe. "Strange though it may seem," says the biographer, "it was probably from this meeting that Pilkington was led to see that his outward religion would not stand in the sight of God."

A personal friend writing of this important time says, "I believe it was in his own room that Pilkington found peace and joy of heart which so characterized him ever afterwards. I know of no human instrument in the matter. I believe he withdrew himself into the desert of loneliness, as it were, alone with God—and prayed until the light came direct from God in His written Word to his soul.... His conversion was not of man, nor by man, but entirely the work of God, the Holy Ghost. This one thing he used to tell me, however, that he thanked God for his faithful friends at Cambridge who, in his own words, 'would not let him alone,' until they saw the grace of God working in his heart. 'The new birth is such a reality that it must produce fruit,' was what he wrote to his mother about conversion."

Work with the C. I. M. abroad appealed to him, but upon writing his parents for their consent, he was asked to postpone it for two years. So, for the next two years, Pilkington was filling the place of temporary master in various schools, but always eagerly laboring for the salvation of the boys with whom he worked.

But again the call came, this time to Africa. Mackay of Uganda was pleading for Cambridge men to come out and form a new base on a new route. Douglas Hooper, a Cambridge man converted at the time of Moody's and Sankey's visit, returned from Africa to make the appeal for Mackay and to return with a party of five or six men. Again Pilkington wrote to his parents for their consent.

"I know you and mother wish me to be a school-master," he writes, "but you would, I know, only wish me to be a good school-master; and when the mind is distracted even by a mistaken idea of duty, it is not possible to produce good work....Neither you, nor mother, no anyone else knows how little satisfaction I have had during the past two years—a continual, ceaseless, restless apprehension, 'You are not where God wants you.' Suppose this is a delusion; the delusion itself is a terrible fact which is spoiling my life, preventing me from doing anything with all my heart, and rendering me more miserable than I can describe; I assure you this is no exaggeration. My daily and hourly longing, 'Only to know that the path I tread is the path marked out by Thee.' You don't know how I long for that knowledge; I believe I should be satisfied to black boots if I knew that was 'the right' way by which the Lord was leading me."

CALL BACK SERIES · VOLUME 1

This time consent was given, and the African party lost no time in getting out to the field. During the long overland march they experienced thirst, fevers oft, dangers from warring tribes, and the loss of several valuable men. Pilkington, athirst for God, plunged into translation work for which he was particularly gifted. He seemed the right man at the right time. Brave Mackay had died while the party were en route, and the need for men was all the greater. But we skip over the months of tedium in learning the native proverbs and idioms for his translation work; months filled with arduous labor and painstaking effort to get the Bible for the Wanganda. Three years had passed, much had been done, but Pilkington was dissatisfied.

Very wisely this discouraged missionary took time to be alone with God in order to candidly and squarely consider his calling. God is ever ready to whisper His secrets to His servants, but they are too busy, too engaged, too occupied. Here on this island, quiet and still, he learned the secret of the indwelling Spirit which transformed his entire life. Thus when he returned on December 7th, 1893, he carried a new Presence with him. The boys he worked with, the Christians of Uganda, and his missionary compatriots all noted the new radiance that shone in his countenance and the fragrance of a fresh influence that in countless little ways spoke more than his words. It is best to describe what happened in his own words.

"If it had not been that God enabled me, after three years in the Mission field, to accept by faith the gift of the Holy Ghost, I should have given up the work. I could not have gone on as I was then. A book by David, the Tamil evangelist, showed me that my life was not right, that I had not the power of the Holy Ghost. I had consecrated myself hundreds of times, but I had not accepted God's gift. I saw now that God commanded me to be filled with the Spirit. Then I read, 'All things, whatsoever ye shall ask in prayer, believing, ye shall receive,' and, claiming this promise, I received the Holy Spirit.

"Another verse which impressed me was John 16:7—'It is expedient for you that I go away: for if I go not away, the Comforter will not come unto you; but if I depart, I will send him unto you.'"

But perhaps the clearest view of the influence on his life of this remarkable experience, may be gained from a letter written by him to his mother.

"Next Sunday is Whit Sunday. Ho, for another Pentecost here, and at home. 'He that believeth on me, out of his belly shall flow rivers (not a stream or a single river) of living water....Greater works than these shall he do; because I go unto the Father.' Where are these rivers and where are these mighty works? We must ask rather, where 'is he that believeth on Him?' Surely He is not unfaithful to a single line of His promise. What wonder that infidelity abounds, when the worst infidelity of all is in our own hearts. What wonder that popery increases, when we have dethroned the Holy Spirit from our hearts. What wonder that Mohammedanism defies us, and still occupies vast fields once held for Christ, when Mohammed's successors can still ask as the false prophet himself did, 'Where, but in Mohammed is the promised Paraclete?' Even the Mohammedans here, ignorant as they are, ask that. Praise be to God, many of our people here can answer, 'In my heart and life.' May abundant fruit of the Spirit in our lives prove our witness true.

"That reminds me that you once wrote as if you thought that I had meant to say that, till eighteen months ago, I had not had the presence or the help of the Holy Spirit in my work. I never meant to convey that impression. I distinguish between the presence of the Holy Spirit with us and in us; our blessed Lord said to His disciples, 'He is with you and shall be in you' (John 14). It is the birthright of every Christian to have the Holy Spirit in him, to be full of the Holy Ghost as St. Paul commanded the Ephesians to be, but I believe that my unbelief and other sins were a hindrance to the Holy Spirit in my heart till about eighteen months ago, when God Himself, I humbly believe, opened, or enabled me to 'open the door,' and He came in, according to His gracious promise, to sup with me, even me, and I with Him."

> "'Tis better far to let Him choose the way that we should take;
> If only we leave our life with Him, He will guide without mistake;
> We, in our blindness, would never choose a pathway dark or rough,
> And so we should never find in Him the God Who is enough.
> In disappointment, trouble, or pain, we turn to the changeless One,
> And prove how faithful, loving and true is God's beloved Son."

—Sel.

ADELIA FISKE
CALLS BACK

"No man should be moved by these afflictions:
for yourselves know that we are appointed thereunto. For verily,
when we were with you, we told you before that we should suffer
tribulation; even as it came to pass, and ye know."
1 THESSALONIANS 3:3-4

SOME YEARS ago, a missionary named Adelia Fiske was in charge of a girls' school in Persia. She had reared her little flock from infancy until they were now nearly grown to young womanhood. They had come to call her "Mother" and had learned from her life's highest ideals. She had forsaken all she had in the world that she might care for this little group of motherless girls.

And then came tragedy. Riots broke out in Persia between the different classes, and hate for foreigners ran high. The town near the little school was filled with fighting and horror. A mob finally burst out of the city, and their torches made grotesque figures on the roadside as they neared the school gate. The missionary, knowing the danger, had refused to leave with the other foreigners in order to protect her girls.

She had gathered them together on this particular night, and the voice of agonizing prayer arose and mingled strangely with the curses and shouts from without. They prayed until the mob finally smashed in the gate and swarmed around the house.

The missionary quietly went outside to try, if possible, to avert the impending disaster. But her voice was lost in the cries and shouts. She was seized bodily and the mob forced their way in on the little group of worshipers. They tied the missionary to the bedpost, and she watched helplessly while they seized the girls and dragged them all off to seeming outrage and ruin.

The next mail boat found a broken-hearted, bitter missionary returning to the United States—her soul darkened with the agony and disappointment of unanswered prayer and the ruin of half a lifetime's work. Her heart remained in this condition nearly a year before she finally opened it to God and let His light shine in again.

Then came God's voice to her soul: "Why are you wasting your time here in bitterness because I did not answer your prayer as you thought best? Do I not have the right to use my prerogative and answer, 'No'? Who are you, to see the end from the beginning, and dictate to Me what is best? Go back to Persia; gather the girls around you and make them vessels unto My honor."

She repented and went. Ultimately every one of the girls, instead of simply being well settled in a home as she had originally planned, became an active missionary to a darkened land.—Henry Harvey

> I know not now, why schemes were spoiled,
> And lofty aspirations foiled;
> I know not now why briar and thorn
> Should mar ambitions nobly born;
> Hereafter I shall know, shall see,
> These very things were best for me.
>
> I know not now why needing aid,
> It did not come, or was delayed.
> I know not now, why burning tears,
> Should fall so often through the years.
> Hereafter I shall know, shall see,
> These very things were best for me.
>
> I know not now why friends should fail,
> And enemies my faith assail.
> I know not now why clouds should burst,
> And flood and tempest do their worst.
> Hereafter, I shall know, shall see,
> These very things were best for me.

I know not now why came that loss,
And why I needed such a cross;
I know not now the need of pain,
Nor why the weakness should remain.
Hereafter I shall know, shall see,
These very things were best for me.

I know not now why sorrow's dart,
Should penetrate and wound my heart.
I know not now why death drew near,
And led away my loved ones dear.
Hereafter I shall know, shall see,
These very things were best for me.

O Master, I believe Thy Word,
Hereafter, I shall know, O Lord,
Shall fully see Thy plan, Thy care,
Thy skill, Thy love beyond compare.
Hereafter I shall know, shall see,
These very things were best for me.

    —A Gardner, in *Message from God*

JOHN ELIOT
CALLS BACK

"Then said I unto them, Ye see the distress that we are in, how Jerusalem lieth waste, and the gates thereof are burned with fire: come, and let us build up the wall of Jerusalem, that we be no more a reproach....Let us rise up and build."

NEHEMIAH 2:17-18

IF ANY ONE seemed to have a special claim to the protecting care of God, one would have thought it would have been John Eliot, the first missionary to the American Indians and also the first Bible translator in the United States. But God has no favorites! John Eliot was to know a heart-rending sorrow when it seemed "failure" could well be written over the work of the past forty years. But this pioneer carried with him an inward Presence and so was not daunted by the prospect. To discover his secret, we must go back to the beginning of his story. Let us rehearse how this English Puritan came to the shores of the New England States in 1631.

John Eliot lived in a beautiful part of England in the county of Hertfordshire. His parents were most particular about the education of their son. He was sent at fourteen to Cambridge where he obtained his B. A. While there, he experienced his first encounter with sorrow when bereaved of both of his parents. But God had a hand upon the young man, and he came to live in the home of the godly Puritan, Thomas Hooker, and consequently "was made to live in Christ." "The Lord said to my dead soul, LIVE!" said Eliot. "And through the grace of God I do live forever. When I came to this blessed family, I saw as never before the power of godliness in its lovely vigor and efficacy."

Foreseeing trouble when persecution broke out against the Puritans in England, Thomas Hooker left England's shores for

Holland. With his host family no longer there for him, Eliot sailed for America, arriving in Boston Nov. 2, 1631. He settled in Roxbury a few miles distant, where he had been invited to preach and teach. Soon another contingent of English emigrants arrived and among them Anne Mumford who became Eliot's wife, theirs being the first recorded marriage in Roxbury.

In the poem "Hiawatha" by Longfellow, a Mohawk Indian foretold the coming of a white missionary to them. Eliot fulfilled this prophecy, for he considered the Indians among the lost tribes of Israel, and so in time, became known as the "Apostle to the Indians."

One day when Eliot was driving past a field, he was roused to great indignation when he noticed a white settler using an Indian to pull his plow. Eliot objected vehemently. To this the farmer declared that the Indian was nothing but a brutal savage. The only condition of his release was to buy him for ten gold pieces. Although Eliot had only eleven, he spontaneously parted with the ten and went home with the Indian. He taught the man, whom he named Job Nebustan, how to read and write, and in turn the Indian acquainted his teacher with the customs and language of his own people. Nebustan was to be a helper in the translation of the first Bible for the Indians.

Eliot was a most prayerful man, and all his labors were saturated with his intercessions. Converts multiplied until they numbered 3,600. These Eliot taught many practical things, setting them to build houses in orderly settlements which others called "praying towns." He also had numbers of full-time native helpers, and it seemed that the little Indian settlement would surely be preserved by God's special oversight. But we must remember that this earth is governed by the prince of this world who opposes vehemently all that would challenge his dominion.

King Philip's war in 1673 brought chaos to all Eliot's efforts. Some Indians had acted without discretion, and so they all were suspected of favoring the white oppressors and were used as scouts, spies, and guides. Many townships were wiped out and Bibles destroyed. The strain of these years proved too much for the new converts and when the war ceased, the work of years lay in ruins. Eliot himself was considered a traitor for caring so very deeply for a people who had massacred and plundered the white man's forts and towns.

John Eliot, now seventy-four, turned once again to the forest in order to help the Indians rebuild those "praying towns" and once again there sprang up from the ruins of the past a new beginning. Difficulties seemed but a spur to this tireless man of prayer, who prayed in the morning, who prayed visiting, who prayed walking, and who taught others to pray.

His dying words were: "My memory, my tongue, my hand, my pen fail me—but my love holds out still." Through gates of pearl the "apostle to the Indians," entered, having passed through "much tribulation." He, John Eliot, will be among those who will join in the heavenly chorus.

> "Thank God for failure, shattered hopes, lost aims,
> And ungained garlands, for He knoweth best.
> 'They also serve who only stand and wait';
> Perchance they also win who seem to fail;
> God's eye sees clearer than our earth-dimmed sight."
>
> —*The Golden Gate of Prayer* by Miller

WILLIAM CAREY CALLS BACK

"He is a chosen vessel unto me, to bear my name
before the Gentiles. ....I will shew him how great things
he must suffer for my name's sake."

ACTS 9:15-16

FAVORITISM on the part of God towards His most honored servants is a theory which needs exploding, for in actual life, as recorded in Christian biography, we find exactly the reverse. The heavens have often appeared as brass, and the silence of an apparently unanswering Heavenly Father, has sorely tried the faith of His finest heroes.

In no life is this principle more apparent than in that of William Carey, often called the Father of Foreign Missions, for he was indeed one of its earliest pioneers. How differently we might have planned out the life of this man, who was given the arduous task of translating the Bible into some of the many dialects of India. We would have doubtless searched about us for the most highly educated linguist available but, instead, God chose a humble cobbler whose brilliant mind was put at His disposal.

Then, for a life-mate of such a man, we would have sought for someone who had complete understanding and sympathy for his life-work and who, of course, would have all the educational qualifications to fit her for such co-partnership with one who was to so greatly affect the whole face of India. But no. Instead we discover that Carey's wife suffered from the mental disease, Monomania, which marked the last thirteen years of her married life by spasms and outbursts. This must have greatly tested her husband who, all the while, was engaged in the exacting work of not only learning the Sanskrit but of providing dictionaries, proof-reading translations, and overseeing the printing.

As if his wife's condition were not a sufficient handicap, we next find that the financial backing, which we would have surely thought his heavenly Father would have supplied for such an ennobling enterprise, was often sadly lacking. Carey had principles which called for a missionary to be self-supporting, working with his own hands while also pursuing his calling. And so it was that, for some years, the family subsisted on meals without meat of any kind, so great was the financial pinch.

Another advantage which we would have deemed essential for such an undertaking, would have been uninterrupted progress and success in the translation work to which Carey had been so unmistakably called. Surely he would have heavy, heavenly insurance coverage against death, earthquake and fire! Instead, all three disasters struck the Serampore Compound where he labored. The year of 1811 was especially trying for that little community, when, out of seven families, death snatched away either wife or child.

This was cause enough for trial of faith, but when, on a March evening, fire swept through the printing establishment, it seemed indeed that providence had failed to smile on the long, arduous years of painstaking translation work and destroyed it in one fell stroke. Ward, the faithful printing manager, was alone at one end of the 250 foot printing plant when the smell of smoke alerted him. Hurrying to the other end of the building which housed the translations, paper supplies, printing type, etc., he saw that, already, devouring flames were beginning their deadly work. Shutting out all drafts, he poured water from the roof and was just about hopeful that he could quench the hungry flames when someone, no one knows who or why, opened a window which had been previously shut. This caused a draft to sweep through the building, fanning the flames until, in a short time, the roof finally toppled in upon the smoldering manuscripts, paper and types. The entire plant stood in ruins.

Carey was away teaching at nearby Calcutta at the time, but when told about the devastating calamity, hurried to the scene. Walking over the smoking ruins, tears filled is eyes as he said: "In one short evening, the labor of years is consumed. How unsearchable are the ways of God. I had lately brought some things to the utmost perfection of which they seemed capable and contemplated the missionary establishment with perhaps too much self-congratulation. The Lord has laid me low that I may look more simply to Him."

How quickly this devoted man of God had discovered the possible purposes of God in chastisement! But, as always, things did "work together for good to them that love God." The news of this disaster created more interest in Europe and America than any previous success had occasioned. In fifty days, £10,000 ($15,000) was raised and Fuller, the home Treasurer, stated, "We must call off the contributions."

A further quote from Carey will reveal the spirit of adventure and faith which inspired prodigious efforts to quickly replace the losses. "I now, however, turn to the bright side. And here I might mention what still remains to us, and merciful circumstances which attend even this stroke of God-rod, but I will principally notice what will tend to cheer the heart of everyone who feels for the cause of God. Our loss, so far as I can see, is reparable in a much shorter time than I should have at first supposed."

Of the Bible translations and grammars, the three partners in the venture wrote: "We found, on making the trial, that the advantages in going over the same ground a second time were so great that they fully counterbalanced the time requisite to be devoted thereto in a second translation." The fire had but improved the translations, and had been the means of producing revised editions of a superior quality.

Some years later, a flood brought an avalanche of mud which swept away a large portion of Carey's botanical gardens which he so highly prized. He had spent long, arduous hours tracing the families and gathering the specimens of plants from all over the world. And this was not all. A cyclone later caused further damage to the conservatories which housed many of his specimens.

But it was not these outward attacks upon the work which were the hardest to bear. Carey suffered far more from the long, drawn-out hostility which some back home showed towards the little Serampore community. No longer did he have his three faithful prayer warriors—Sutcliffe, Fuller and Ryland, to hold the ropes but, now that they had arrived at the point of public acceptance and apparent prosperity, new committees made up of more sophisticated members had taken their place. Misunderstandings continued. Letters of explanation about a multitude of details were demanded of Carey, letters which he most painstakingly albeit grudgingly wrote, for he felt the attacks upon them were petty and ill-timed.

Answering one letter in which the writer accused the missionaries of wasting money, Carey wrote:

"I might have had large possessions, aye, and kept them lawfully, too. I labored hard for all that I have, but I have not kept for myself or family what was justly mine. I have given my all, except what I ate, drank, and wore, to the cause of missions. Dr. Marshman has done the same, and so did Mr. Ward. I am so poor that I can scarcely lay by a sum monthly to relieve one or two indigent relatives in England. Dr. Marshman is as poor as I am. Where is the pomp that is complained of?"

We read that Carey's faith triumphed in the last three years of his life. "Blow succeeded blow" as his biographer put it, "that the fine gold of his trust and his humility and his love might be seen to be purer."

The final blow was the financial loss of all the funds of the Serampore College and Mission. The firm with which they had deposited funds suddenly failed. All was swept away. The three partners—Carey, Marshman and Ward—had contributed the sum of

£90,000 out of their own earnings to the cause of God in India. Now Carey died so poor that in order to execute his final will, his library had to be sold to give a small sum to his son. And yet, to one of his companions in labor he said a few days prior to his death, "I have no fear. I have no doubts. I have not a wish unsatisfied."

TWO MINISTERS
CALL BACK

"Plans pertain to the heart of man,
but the last word is from the Lord."

PROVERBS 16:1
—from a translation

"They assayed to go into Bithynia:
but the Spirit suffered them not"

ACTS 16:7

"Did I show levity...or do I plan after the flesh,
that the yea with me must be always yea, and the nay always nay,
as it is with a man of the world who makes his plans independently
of God's overruling of them?"

2 CORINTHIANS 1:17
-paraphrase of Chrysostom

A **FALL** from a camel! A very serious illness! Could these untoward happenings in the lives of two of the four godly ministers sent out on a mission to survey open doors possibly be accounted for as from God?

When the Church Committee in Scotland had outlined the route for their four representatives to follow, they in their human short-sightedness left out Hungary because they considered the current political set-up unfavorable to their mission. So the Lord of the Harvest had to step in. He alone knew of the secret prayers that for seven long years had been ascending to His Throne of Grace. Men or committees are not "Lords of the Harvest," and that is why so many of their efforts are abortive. We reason by human calculations and leave out the "desert way" where prepared souls are ripe for reaping.

If God's messengers are to be directed to the corner of the harvest-field, their human course must be arrested somehow. A fall from a camel, or an illness, or an accident on the road, or an unexpected delay, might well be the sign-post of the Lord of the Harvest pointing in a different direction than our best judgments would direct. Let us ask God the reason for the upset of our plans instead of giving in to our frustration.

Read the amazing account, as given by A. T. Pierson in *The New Acts of the Apostles*, of how man's plans were foiled for a better one:

"In the recently published memoir of Adolph Saphir, there is put on record one of the countless instances of divine administration of missions, which we cite because of the many-sided lesson taught.

"It is the story of how the mission for the Jews was established in Pesth, Hungary. Prayer is the key to every new mystery in this series of marvels. First, the father of this movement was Mr. R. Woodrow, of Glasgow, whose private diary shows whole days of fasting and prayer on behalf of Israel. The next step was the appointment of a deputation, in 1838, consisting of those four remarkable men, Doctors Keith and Black, with Andrew Bonar and McCheyne, to visit lands where the Jews dwelt, and select fields for missions to this neglected people.

"The intolerance of the Austrian government seemed to shut the door to any work within its dominions, and so, notwithstanding the large Jewish population there resident, Hungary was not embraced in the plan of visitation. But God did not propose that this land should be longer passed by; and He, by mysterious links, joined the plan of the deputation to His own purposes for Hungary.

"Dr. Black slipped from his camel's back as they were crossing from Egypt to Palestine, and the seemingly trifling accident proved sufficiently serious to change the homeward route of Dr. Black and Dr. Keith, by way of the Danube. As they passed through Pesth, they made some inquiries as to the Jews there to be found, little knowing what unseen Hand was leading 'the blind by a way that they knew not.'

"The Archduchess Maria Dorothea, then residing in the Prince Palatine's palace, had some years previously been led, by a death in her family, to seek solace in the Bible, where 'she met Jesus.' She was, by the imperial law, forced to bring up her children in the Roman Catholic Church; but as she had found the truth, she taught them, with much prayer, the way of faith, and, in her solitude, yearned and besought of God that a Christian friend and counselor might be sent to her.

"In a window of her boudoir, which overlooked the city with its hundred thousand people, day by day, for seven years, she had poured out her soul in prayer to God for someone to carry the true Gospel to those around her; at times, in agony, stretching out imploring hands to God for at least one messenger of the cross to come to Hungary.

"The year of 1840 came, with Drs. Keith's and Black's providential visit to Pesth, and Dr. Keith's almost fatal illness there—and just at this time the Archduchess was strongly and strangely impressed that a stranger was about to arrive who would bring a peculiar blessing to the Hungarians she loved. There was one fortnight particularly, when, night after night, she awoke at the same hour, with a vivid sense that something was about to take place which was to bring her relief. And when at last she heard that Dr. Keith was in town dangerously ill of cholera, she said to herself, 'This is what was to happen to me.' And from that hour her sleep was no longer broken.

"She went to the bedside of the prostrate stranger, and with her own hands ministered to his wants; and, as he became better, told him of her longings and prayers, acquainted him with the state of the Hungarian Jews, and assured him that if the Church of Scotland would plant a mission in Pesth, she would throw about it all possible guards. And so it came to pass that, in the very field which the deputation purposely left out of all their schemes, God brought about, by link upon link of His inscrutable providence, the famous mission associated with the name of 'Rabbi Duncan,' and which was the means of giving, to the Church of Christ, Adolph Saphir.

"Thus came the Protestant Gospel into Buda-Pesth and by what a series of divine leadings! A man's prayer in Glasgow, a woman's prayer in Hungary, a seeming accident on desert sand, a change of route, an almost fatal illness, a visit of an Archduchess—who shall dare to doubt that the Hungarian mission was a tree of God's planting! Who can wonder that, as the first missionaries went to this new field, they 'felt wafted along by the breath of prayer, and had, from the very beginning, a mysterious expectation of success!'"

"God never is before His time and never is too late."

DAVID HILL
CALLS BACK

"Our light affliction, which is but for a moment, worketh for us a far more exceeding and eternal weight of glory; While we look not at the things which are seen, but at the things which are not seen."

2 CORINTHIANS 4:17-18

Dᴀᴠɪᴅ ʜɪʟʟ, an Englishman of culture and refinement, went out as a Methodist missionary to China. He found that the task of spreading the Gospel of Jesus Christ among proud Confucianists taxed his endurance and faith to the limit. Let him give us an insight into his struggles, for they will help us to understand the fearful price which has had to be paid when we invade the devil's kingdom. From a book, *How David Hill Followed Christ* by J. E. Hellier, we quote several excerpts from his letters which give us a glimpse of his difficulties:

"'The opposition of the literary classes is deadly and devilish and will not be satisfied without something like deadly and devilish manifestation of it....We have as yet scarcely made ourselves felt in our assaults on the Confucian citadel, but when we do and have to come into direct and hand-to-hand fight with these upper classes of the people we shall feel that if true now that "our wrestling is not against flesh and blood, but against the principalities, against the powers, against the world-rulers of this darkness, against the spiritual hosts of wickedness in heavenly places," it is felt to be ten-fold more true then; but the "weapons of our warfare are...mighty through God to the pulling down of strong holds," so we have nothing to fear ....

"'So I was debarred the pleasure of replying to the vilification of this follower of the great Confucius. Such is a fair sample of at least five-sixths of the literary class in China, and nothing but Divine power and Divine love brought to bear upon them by the Divine Spirit

Himself can bring these men to their right mind. Oh! Pray that we may receive the Spirit, for we are good for nothing if He be not present with us.'"

As in David Hill's experience, tribulation and disappointments so often dog the footsteps of the true saint, while less godly men triumph in their building programs and seem to prosper in their labors. Did we but know it is these very trials which occur in our work for God that are permitted to try us, for God's ends are different from ours. We are weighing the work of our hands which is but for a moment measured on the scale of man's success, while God is weighing our character, so that we may be of use in His eternal plan for the ages to come.

It is only later in life that we learn that our heavenly Father is far more interested in what we are than the work we do for Him. This time on earth is a training ground for His faithful followers. God is looking toward a future which we do not see, when we shall reign with Him and assist in governing His future Kingdom. Jesus will have a glorious reign, and those He chooses shall have come through great tribulation and have been truly tried and tested as to their loyalties to Him.

We are so focused on our work for Him that we judge His silences as denials or even displeasure, when really He is putting iron into the very fiber of our spiritual being, and patience, affliction, and opposition are actively working to produce the likeness of His Son within us.

David Hill met such frustrating delays in his chapel-building, that it aged him considerably as his biographer relates:

"David Hill longed for that chapel as an essential to the success of the Gospel in Wuchang. He required a good site and a good position, and the waiting and delay not only disappointed him, but tried his faith and patience to the uttermost. Why the Lord, Who ruleth all things by the word of His power, withheld and delayed the answer to his prayers and his heart's desire, he could not tell. His way was hid in darkness, and again he judged himself unworthy and accused himself needlessly. He grew, indeed, morbid, and believed that the Chinese were plotting against him, though no evidence of such a plot was ever discovered.

"Living day by day to encounter dislike and hostility, frustrated in his most ardent hopes and desires, he passed through a time of trial and suffering impossible to describe. It was necessary, no doubt. The Lord, through this experience, led him to understand his hard and difficult work, and to cast his soul more than ever on His unseen, eternal love and power, and his loving, enduring soul became strong at last to bear contempt, dislike, suspicion, hatred, and the foregoing of his own plans and purposes, that in him and by him the will of the Lord Jesus might be perfectly done ....

"The long, sorrowful conflict came to an end, but it left its marks on him. It brought the first sprinkling of gray hairs among the brown, and in his letters we hear a deeper note. Take, for instance, these words, addressed to his old friend, Rev. John Norton Vine: 'I have been much struck with the "strivings" St. Paul experienced. Col. 1:29; 2:1.' He read of these 'strivings' in the light of his own experience, and he entered into fellowship with the Apostle's agonizing conflicts, for he had felt the same."

A. B. Simpson also experienced these manifold temptations while doing work for the Master and wrote this hymn which has been such a blessing to us:

> Oft there comes a gentle whisper o'er me stealing
>> When my trial and my burden seem too great,
> Like the sweet-voiced bells of evening softly pealing,
>> It is saying to my spirit—"Only wait."
>
> When I cannot understand my Father's leading,
>> And it seems to be but hard and cruel fate;
> Still I hear that gentle whisper ever pleading,
>> "God is working, God is faithful—Only wait."

When the promise seems to linger, long delaying,
    And I tremble lest perhaps it comes too late,
Still I hear that sweet-voiced angel ever saying,
    "Tho' it tarry, it is coming—Only wait."

When I see the wicked prosper in their sinning,
    And the righteous often pressed by some dark strait,
I remember this is only the beginning
    And I whisper to my spirit—"Only wait."

JAMES McCONKEY
CALLS BACK

"They assayed to go...but the Spirit suffered them not."

ACTS 16:7

JAMES McCONKEY came to be called "The Apostle of the Surrendered Life" after bereavement, unexpectedly entering his family, opened to him a door of unmeasured blessing. From an article in the *Alliance Witness* we learn the details of that thwarted ambition which proved to be a blessing in disguise:

"There were many purposeful young men at Princeton University in those days, and perhaps none was more purposeful than James H. McConkey. Every year, he became more certain that there was no career for him except law. He soon began to make a reputation for himself by his public speaking in Whig Hall, and his succeeding Woodrow Wilson as president of a campus society confirmed him in his purpose. Added to his speaking ability was a deep-rooted respect and love for law itself. Life stretched before him as a field of battle in which he would gain victory after victory.

"But 'the best laid schemes o' mice and men gang aft a-gley.' Toward the end of his last year, the death of his father changed his whole prospect. As the eldest son, he faced the responsibility of supporting an invalid mother, seven sisters, and a young brother of twelve. Besides, there was a formidable debt. He never could do it all and still endure the proverbial two years of starvation that law exacted. There was nothing for him to do but take up his father's business and exchange his dream career for a mundane job.

"He was a Christian, but now he began to feel his need of God as never before. He also saw the need for Bible study, so he began to study in his room at night. Gradually this became his chief joy.

BOOK 3 · FRUSTRATION

"Gradually, too, the atmosphere began to change, as if it had taken on a faintly rosy tint like an early sunrise. More and more he became sensitive to casual things—his mother's greeting in the evenings, for instance, with eyes full of loving appreciation. All the concerns of the family were now his concern. There was no time for self-pity. Love was driving it out; reality had broken through. Christ became nearer to him than breathing. Later he said that he had not been able to hand over to Him his work and his very self for eternity until he heard an unknown man say one evening in prayer, 'Lord, we know we can trust the Man who died for us.' The verse around which he lived his whole life thereafter was Romans 12:1. His body was presented on the altar and kept there.

"Fifteen years passed in which he seized on God's will daily. By that time the family debt had been paid, the mother had died and the rest of the children had married. The neighbors little suspected the spiritual revolution which had taken place in that young life, in the man who later would be called 'The Apostle of the Surrendered Life.' Now that he was absolved of family responsibilities and had more free time he found himself wondering what he should do next. He felt that perhaps the next step would be a regular evening Bible class; so he asked the Lord simply whether it was or not, and promised that he would accept the first invitation he received.

"A few days later a note came from a small group in a railroad YMCA. It said that they had been praying for a teacher to come to them one evening a week, and all felt sure that he was God's choice. That was James McConkey's leading, and for years he had an itinerary all along the Pennsylvania Railroad near his home in Wrightsville, Pennsylvania. As he kept studying, the Lord continued to bring invitations, including some to speak in summer conferences.

"His next leading was to write simple, devotional messages which he had already tried out in classes and submit them to *The Sunday*

School Times and other periodicals. Then letters of appreciation began to come in from individuals and groups who wanted these messages in booklet form. It was evident that there was need of guidance now for a move. It came, and he rented a two-room office in the Bessemer Building in Pittsburgh. There the booklets and the subsequent books were sent out all over the United States to those who longed to know God in a deeper way. Some of these have been translated into eighteen languages.

"The sowing of the seed was done quietly and unostentatiously, but there were proofs of the harvest whenever those who had been reading began to discuss the great truths they were nurturing in their hearts, truths which the Holy Spirit had printed indelibly won their hearts as they read. Invitations to speak were by now making a problem that he had not anticipated; but his old practice of going back to God with 'Not my will, but Thine, be done' had become a fixed habit. No longer was there the struggle of the first years. Having 'the mind of God' was required before any decision was made. Then wild horses could not have dragged him away from it. And what about the law career? There were no regrets. Many times he was heard to say, 'Law is a noble profession, but it was not the life's work God had for me.' There was no question about the benefit he had received from his legal training, in both his writing and his speaking. What if he had failed to accept each change in his career, seeing only a part of the whole, day by day? What if he had missed his life's work? What if he had never followed Him 'Who hath saved us, and called us with an holy calling,…which was given us in Christ Jesus before the world began'? Ask the thousands who have read his books and booklets."

Another incident in the life of James McConkey will mean much to some who have passed through similar circumstances and may not as yet have found the secret as he did:

"In my early life I entered a partnership with a friend in the wholesale ice business. Both of us were young men, and we embarked all we had, and considerably more, in the business. We met with disappointments. For two seasons in succession our ice was swept away by winter freshets. Things had come to a serious pass. It seemed very necessary that we should have ice in the winter of which I now speak.

"The weather became very cold. The ice formed and grew thicker and thicker, until it was fit to gather. I remember the joy that came into our hearts one afternoon when there came an order for thousands of tons of ice which would lift us entirely out from our financial stress.

"Not long before, God had let me see the truth of committal. He showed me that it was His will that I should commit my business to Him and trust Him with it absolutely. As best I knew how, I had done so. I never dreamed what testing was coming. So I lay down that Saturday night in quietness.

"At midnight there came an ominous sound—rain. By morning it was pouring in torrents. Yellow streaks of water crept over the ice. Water at flood stage had swept away our ice twice before. By noon the storm was raging in all its violence. By afternoon I had come into a great spiritual crisis. By mid-afternoon I had come face to face with the tremendous fact that deep in my heart was rebellion against God.

"That rebelliousness seemed to develop in a suggestion in my heart like this, "You gave all to God. You say you are going to trust God with your business. This is the way He requites you. Your business will be swept away, and tomorrow you will come into a place of desperate financial stress." My heart grew bitter at the thought that God should take away my business when I wanted it only for legitimate purposes.

"Then another Voice seemed to speak: 'My child, did you mean it when you said you would trust Me? Can you not trust Me in the dark as well as in the light? Would I do anything or suffer anything to come into your life which will not work out good for you?'

"Still back and forth, with ever-increasing intensity, waged one of the greatest spiritual battles of my life. At the end of two hours, by the grace of God, I was able to cry out, 'Take the business, take the ice, take everything; only give me the supreme blessing of an absolutely submitted will to Thee.' And then peace.

"The storm was still beating upon my ice, but it seemed to make no difference whether it rained or ceased. Then and there I discovered that the secret of anxious care was not in surroundings, but in the failure of allowing life and will to be wholly given up to Him. That night I lay down to rest in perfect peace, but with the rain pouring torrents upon my field of ice, and with every prospect that my business would lie in wreck the next morning—but it did not. By midnight came the sound of wind. By morning the bitterest blizzard of the year was upon us. By evening the mercury had fallen to the zero point. In a few days we harvested the finest ice we ever had.

"God did not want my ice. But He did want my will, and my absolute trust in Him; when that was settled, He gave back the ice, blessed the business, and led me on until He guided me into the place He had for me from the beginning—that of a teacher of His Word."

—from *The Surrendered Life* by James H. McConkey

> He was better to me than all my hopes;
>> He was better than all my fears.
> He made a bridge of my broken works,
>> And a rainbow of my tears.
> The billows that guarded my sea-girt path
>> But carried my Lord on their crest.
> When I dwell on the days of my wilderness march,
>> I can lean on His love for the rest.
>
> He emptied my hands of my treasured store,
>> And His covenant love revealed,
> There was not a wound in my aching heart
>> But the balm of His breath hath healed.

Oh, tender and true was the chastening sore,
   In wisdom that taught and tried,
Till the soul that He sought was trusting in Him
   And nothing on earth beside.

—Unknown

ROLAND BINGHAM
CALLS BACK

"They that sow in tears shall reap in joy."
PSALMS 126:5

"We are troubled on every side, yet not distressed."
2 CORINTHIANS 4:8

"ON MY RETURN the whole expedition was written off as a failure. What was there to show for the effort? Nothing, but two graves." Thus Roland Bingham summed up the first effort to evangelize the Sudan in Africa for Christ. God chooses the weak things with which to work His will, and He had that qualification in this man.

The instigator and burden-bearer was a little Scottish Canadian woman who had already given one daughter to the mission field in China. Her eldest son, fired by the burden and vision of his intercessory mother, offered to go out to that needy area where 60-90 million Africans were without one missionary. Walter Gowans sought the aid of Missionary Societies in both Canada and America and found none willing to finance or back such an undertaking. He then tried Great Britain with the same results.

Dr. Bingham, founder of the S. I. M., years later said, "All sought to dissuade us from our purpose as, long years before, others had sought to dissuade David Livingstone. Prayer brought to us the same conviction that had been his. 'I will open up Central Africa to the Gospel or die in the attempt.' Therein is laid bare the secret of the extraordinary success that has attended the Sudan Interior Mission."

But to boldly confront this large area with its teeming population was to challenge the powers of darkness. The first mission seemed a signal failure. Roland Bingham, sick with malaria, was ordered home, and alone he returned to Canada, having left his two brave companions, Walter Gowans and Tom Kent, in lonely graves. Frustration seemed to dog every step and the forces of darkness and evil appeared to triumph.

Walter Gowans, who laid down his life for Sudan, had said these words the year he sailed for Africa: "Our success in this enterprise means nothing less than the opening of the Sudan for the Gospel. Our failure at the most—nothing more than the death of two or three deluded fanatics! But if we fail, it will be our fault through lack of faith. God is faithful. He faileth not. Still, even death is not failure. His purposes are accomplished. He uses deaths as well as lives to the furtherance of His cause. After all, is it not worth a venture? Sixty million souls are at stake."

"My faith was being shaken to the very foundation," wrote Roland Bingham, the lone survivor. "I had gone out, as I thought, trusting in promises of healing that seemed plain, clear and explicit in the Bible, and yet I had left buried in the Sudan two of the most faithful Christians whom I had ever met. Had the promises failed? Why should those most anxious to carry out the Lord's commands and to give the Gospel to millions in darkness be cut off right at the beginning of their career?

"Many questions faced me. It did not occur to me that my interpretations of the promises had been mistaken. Was the Bible merely an evolution of human thought, even biased thought, or was it a divine revelation? For months the struggle over the great issue went on before I was finally brought back to the solid rock. In the fall of that year I returned to Canada. I had no Board to report to and no financial accounting to give as I had never solicited any money for our expedition. I was now convinced of the need of some form of organization and of a home base."

In 1900, at the close of the first seven years since his first attempt, Roland Bingham set out again on a second venture with two other young men. "When I landed," wrote Bingham, "I found the missionaries in Lagos more than ever out of sympathy with my plans. They did not hesitate to express themselves to the two young men I had brought with me. Within three weeks from the time we arrived I was once more stricken down with malaria and taken to the government hospital. The doctor ordered me home and I was carried on a stretcher to a 'branch boat' and transferred to the ocean vessel anchored out at sea.

"My young companions assured me that they would carry on, but discouraged by the dark picture painted by the missionaries at Lagos, they followed me home on the next boat. It would have been easier for me, perhaps, had I died in Africa, for on the homeward journey I died another death. Everything seemed to have failed, and when, while regaining strength in Britain, a fateful cable reached me with word that my two companions were arriving shortly, I went through the darkest period of my whole life."

The intercessory prayers of Mrs. Gowans held Dr. Bingham steadfast so that a third party of four set out again for the interior of the Sudan. But again failure seemed to dog the efforts to open this field. Two of the party of four were sent back home ill, never to return. A third found a grave there, but the fourth remained and began Bible translation work which proved of invaluable help in the future opening of the work there. The discovery of the bark of the cinchona tree provided the quinine which was to make such a difference in the treatment of malaria which hitherto had proved fatal in so many cases.

"When Heaven is about to confer a great office on a man," said Mencius, the Chinese sage, some two thousand years ago, "it always first exercises his mind and soul with suffering, and his body to hunger, and exposes him to extreme poverty, and baffles all his undertakings. By these means it stimulates his mind, hardens his nature, and enables him to do acts otherwise not possible to him."

Roland Bingham, after fourteen years of baffled hopes, foiled endeavors, and thwarted plans, finally emerged into a period of promise which he termed, "The Beginning of Fruitfulness."

The Sudan Interior Mission grew to become one of the largest, interdenominational missionary societies with 1,300 missionaries and 133 stations among seventy-one tribes in ten African countries. But the price had been paid by the largely unknown pioneers who had fallen and had been buried alone as corns of wheat in the vast field of Sudan.

> Will not the End explain
> The crossed endeavor, earnest purpose foiled,
> The strange bewilderment of good work spoiled,
> The clinging weariness, the inward strain,
> Will not the End explain?
>
> Meanwhile He comforteth
> Them that are losing patience; 'tis His way.
> But none can write the words they hear Him say,
> For men to read; only they know He saith
> Kind words, and comforteth.
>
> Not that He doth explain
> The mystery that baffleth; but a sense
> Husheth the quiet heart, that far, far hence
> Lieth a field set thick with golden grain,
> Wetted in seedling days by many a rain.
> The End, it will explain.
>
> —Unknown

It is doubtful whether God can bless a man greatly until He has hurt him deeply.—A. W. Tozer

"True faith never knows defeat. It triumphs in every seeming overthrow; overpowered, it conquers; killed, it comes to life; buried, it rises again.

"The ideas of triumph are very different from those of the world. It sees occasion to exult in what a worldly religion would call failure. What would be thought of a man at the present day who, with such a career as St. Paul's, claimed in every battle to be victorious? He might consider himself fortunate if he escaped being shut up as insane.

"At Damascus the Jews lay in wait to kill Paul. At Antioch the chief men of the city expelled him from their coasts. At Lystra, after seeing the miracle at Corinth, he was beaten before the judgment seat. At Ephesus the whole city was thrown into a tumult on his account. At Jerusalem he was bound with thongs and barely escaped with his life. Yet he exclaimed as if he had enjoyed uninterrupted prosperity, 'Now thanks be unto God, which always causeth us to triumph in Christ.'"—B. T. Roberts

FRANCES RIDLEY HAVERGAL
CALLS BACK

"Behold, he breaketh down, and it cannot be built again:
he shutteth up a man, and there can be no opening."

JOB 12:14

THREE VERY RELIGIOUS men sought to comfort a saint of God who was being lashed by one succession of trials after another. Instead, they troubled him considerably because they concluded that he was being punished by the Almighty. The story of that severe provocation can be read in the Book of Job. There are, however, many such comforters today who take it as an omen of God's disfavor when acute and bitter suffering comes to a professed child of God. They have never learned of God's chastening process in which He trains His own for future work in His coming kingdom.

How varied are the means God uses to train these saints during their sojourn here on earth! We all are familiar with that well known "consecration" hymn written by Frances Havergal: "Take My Life and Let It Be." We would have naturally expected God to hedge in such a dedicated writer, poet, and composer from all frustration and disappointment. Not so! Several disasters overtook Miss Havergal in her career as a Christian writer. We have her own reactions written by herself in a letter at the time:

"I have just had such a blessing in the shape of what would have been only two months ago a really bitter blow to me. And now it is actual accession of joy, because I find that it does not even touch me!

"I was expecting a letter from America, enclosing $70.00 now due to me, and possibly news that 'Bruey' was going on like steam and my other book pressingly wanted. The letter has come, and, instead of all this, my publisher has failed in the universal crash. He holds my written promise to publish only with him as the condition of his launching me. So this is not simply a little loss, but an end of all my American prospects of either cash, influence, or fame, at any rate for a long time to come.

"Two months ago this would have been a real trial to me, for I had built a good deal on my American prospects; now 'Thy will be done' is not a sigh but a song!"

The next year another more serious set-back came just when she was full of spiritual vitality and planning a heavy schedule of writing. Her sister, Marie, gives the details of the fire which destroyed her manuscripts:

"Very patiently had she prepared for press many sheets of manuscript music in connection with the Appendix to *Songs of Grace and Glory*. Well do I remember that day it was completed. We were at home and she came down from her study with a large roll of post, and with holiday glee exclaimed, 'There it is all done! And now I am free to write a book.'

"Only a week passed, when the mail brought her the news: 'Messrs. Henderson's premises were burned down this morning about four o'clock. We fear the whole of the stereotypes of your musical edition are destroyed as they were busy printing it. It will be many days before the debris will be sufficiently cooled to ascertain how the stereotype plates stand.'

"Further news confirmed the loss: 'Your musical edition, together with the paper sent for printing it, has been totally destroyed.' On the same sheet Frances wrote to her sisters in Worcestershire: 'The signification hereof to me is that, instead of having finished my whole work, I have to begin again *de novo*, and I shall probably have at least six months of it. The greater part of the manuscript of my Appendix is simply gone, for I had kept no copy whatever, and have not even a list of the tunes. Every chord of my own will have to be reproduced;

every chord of anyone else re-examined and revised. All through my previous *Songs of Grace and Glory* work, and my own books, I had always taken the trouble to copy off every correction on to a duplicate proof, but finding I never gained any practical benefit, I did not as I considered it waste time in this case.

"'Of most of the new work, which has cost me the winter's labor, I have not even a memorandum left, having sent everything to the printers. However, it is so clearly "Himself hath done it," that I can only say "Thy way not mine, O Lord."

"'I only tell you how the case stands, not as complaining of it, only because I want you to ask that I may do what seems drudgery quite patiently, and that I may have health enough for it, and that He may overrule it for good. It may be that He has more to teach me before He sets me free to write the two books which I hoped to have begun directly. Thus I am cut off from the bright stream of successful writing, and stopped in all my own plans for this spring....If I did not rejoice in letting Him to do what He will with me, when He thus sends me such very marked and individual dealing, I should feel that my desire for sanctification, for His will to be done in me, had been merely nominal, or fancied and not real.'"

So often Christian activities prove a barrier to our very closest communion with the Lord. So God in love permits frustrations to come to draw us close to Himself. The events quoted above were to be used to do just this in Miss Havergal's life, and there were lessons learned which she could never have learned if her own plans had had a successful issue. Like Job, Frances Havergal came to appreciate that loving but chastening Hand which had checked her undue eagerness to "do" rather than "be." Again, she shares with a friend the blessing she received through these frustrating circumstances:

"No, it has not been all for Him of late. I don't mean anything definite, but breaches in the enclosure, made not by any outward foe or even 'the religious world,' but by self, which I wanted to be crushed out of me, that He might take its place wholly. I think that has been the 'something between,' and it has dimmed not only the inner brightness, but the free-hearted testimony. It is so utterly horrid not to have been ALL for Him. I do feel ready to say, 'sinners of whom I am chief,' and no expressions of self-bemoaning are too strong for me. I am glad He did not set me free to write. I distinctly believe it to be His holding me back from teaching before I am taught!"

NOTABLE MEN
CALL BACK

"They sacrifice unto their net, and burn incense unto their drag; because by them their portion is fat, and their meat plenteous."

HABAKKUK. 1:16

"Master, we have toiled all the night, and have taken nothing: nevertheless at thy word I will let down the net."

LUKE 5:5

IN ORDER to have the abiding secret of power we must consent to seeming failure for Jesus. I do not know how that thought may strike you, but if you look at the crises events in the Bible and into the lives of people of great faith, you will find over and over again that the sweep of power turned on the pivot of a perfect willingness to fail utterly in the eyes of the world. Those who work with God cannot be failures, but there are times when from our standpoint and feeling everything seems to fail utterly, and our quiet acquiescence in such apparent failure for Jesus' sake, while it closes the valve on the creature side, opens the divine side for the inflow of the energy that moves the universe.

It is very easy for even sanctified souls to become attached to their work and to want it to succeed as their work. It is so easy for devoted persons running camp meetings, conventions, faith homes, missions, or any kind of philanthropic or spiritual enterprise, to become greatly attached to the enterprise itself, and to have an overweening desire for success. But a close analysis of the heart will often reveal the fact that the craving for success is because we are putting ourselves into the affair, and the Holy Ghost Who searches all things, finds out the terrible secret that after all it is self that wants success.

Now, in order that God may get all the glory, He must blister the fair face of seeming success, make us die to ourselves in our work, and then He can accomplish greater results than we dream. Jesus does not want us to get wedded to His work instead of to Him.

—From *Spiritual Power* by G. D. Watson

"If all the results of my ministry can be statistically stated, it is a dire failure," said the renowned preacher, G. Campbell Morgan. And speaking of Ruth—her lofty consecration in leaving her own country and kindred, and then her subsequent marriage with Boaz, bearing Obed, the forerunner of the royal line of David—he said, "They did not live to reap the ultimate harvest of their fidelity, but God found a foothold in the man and woman of faith, and in their united lives. That is the principle of which I think we need to be reminded, in order to encourage our hearts in the midst of work.

"Paul was a saint, cribbed, cabined, and confined in prison. It is impossible to read his letters without being conscious of a certain amount of restlessness as he made appeal to his loved ones, 'Remember my bonds!' A man whose motto was, 'The Regions Beyond,' whose piercing eye saw the far distances, and who was profoundly conscious of the value of the evangel, who knew and wrote, 'I am a debtor…I am ready,' was yet imprisoned, and had to content himself with writing letters.

"Today those letters are of greater value than all his work. He did not know that presently they would be gathered together, and would constitute the great exposition of the evangelical faith for all the centuries.

"Remember, that of the work you do today you cannot see the issue, if it is work wrought by faith in God. It may be in the great city of London, or in some hidden hamlet among the hills that your life will be lived, small, unknown, never published, never noticed either in the religious or irreligious press, and yet you may be God's foothold for things of which you cannot dream, which if told you now, you would not possibly believe."—From *Ruth*

"We have got more from Paul's prison-house than from his visit to the third heavens."—A. Bonar

> Nature's least worthy growths have quickest spring
> And soonest answering service readiest meed
> And undiscerning glory's shining wing
> Lights earliest on all ill-deserving head.
> Winter o'er autumn-scattered wheat doth fling
> A white oblivion that keeps warm the seed;
> And wisest thought needs deepest burying,
> Before its ripe effect begins to breed.
> Therefore, O spiritual seeds-man, cast
> With unregretful hand thy rich grain forth,
> Nor think thy word's regenerating birth
> Dead, that so long lies locked in human breast.
> Time, slow to foster things of lesser worth,
> Broods o'er thy work, and God permits no waste.
>
> —William Caldwell Roscoe

The following advice from the pen of George Bowen, a missionary of many years in India, is most timely for all Christian workers:

"Christians often err in estimating fruit. Success is often latent, coming slowly to light, and that which is more rapid and conspicuous may turn out at last to have been the opposite of success. He that is sincerely bent on bringing forth much fruit to Christ will rest with satisfaction in this conception alone, namely, that the favor of God is fruit. Am I doing that which has the approbation of the almighty Disposer of all? If I am, then I am bringing forth the best possible fruit. It will appear in His own good time, though it should be a thousand years hence.

"One man insists on seeing his fruit, and God gives way to him and lets him have what he seeks; he sees his work prospering in his hands, but, unhappily, it does not endure. There is in the end the bitterness of disappointment.

"Another asks but one thing—that he may please to the uttermost Him Who has called him to be His servant. He is willing to wait in apparent sterility until God shall give the increase. He knows that God is the AUTHOR OF ALL TRUE FRUIT AND HAS THE ABSOLUTE CONTROL OF ALL RESOURCES, AND CAN ACCOMPLISH by the wave of His hand the renovation of the world. Accordingly he puts his seed into the hand of God, sure that, in the best of times, he will see the best of harvests. Let us abide in Christ, bury ourselves in Him, be found in Him. 'Except a corn of wheat fall into the ground and die, it abideth alone; but if it die, it bringeth forth much fruit.'"

Success is simply finding out what God's will is for us, and then doing it. This has meant that God has sent men to sow the seed where no eye observed and no immediate rewards were realized, while others were sent to reap that upon which they had bestowed no labor.

William Burns seemed an example of this principle. When he took over the pastorate of R. M. McCheyne, a revival of tremendous proportions followed. McCheyne had sowed in tears, organizing many prayer meetings in his large parish. But the Synod had sent him with three other ministers on a fact-finding mission and while he was absent, Rev. Burns reaped the harvest.

But later Burns was sent to a field in China where he was the sower, and he labored arduously with no visible results. "One soweth and another reapeth that both may rejoice together." Success is in sowing or reaping in that portion of the harvest-field which God appoints.

> Then learn to scorn the praise of men,
> And learn to lose with God;
> For Jesus won the world through shame,
> And beckons thee His road.
> God's glory is a wondrous thing,
> Most strange in all its ways,

And, of all things on earth, least like
    What men agree to praise.

As He can endless glory weave
    From what men reckon shame,
In His own world He is content
    To play a losing game.

                —F. W. Faber

www.ingramcontent.com/pod-product-compliance
Lightning Source LLC
Chambersburg PA
CBHW021357090426
42742CB00009B/899